D0600200

soups and breads

Published in 2008 by Murdoch Books Pty Limited.
www.murdochbooks.com.au

Murdoch Books Australia
Pier 8/9, 23 Hickson Road
Millers Point NSW 2000
Phone: + 61 (0) 2 8220 2000
Fax: + 61 (0) 2 8220 2558

Murdoch Books UK Limited
Erico House, 6th Floor
93–99 Upper Richmond Road
Putney, London SW15 2TG
Phone: + 44 (0) 20 8785 5995
Fax: + 44 (0) 20 8785 5985

Chief Executive: Juliet Rogers
Publishing Director: Kay Scarlett

Concept & Art Direction: Sarah Odgers
Design: Jacqueline Duncan
Project Manager: Rhiain Hull
Editor: Jacqueline Blanchard
Photographer: Jared Fowler
Stylist: Cherise Koch
Production: Kita George
Food preparation: Alan Wilson
Introduction text: Leanne Kitchen
Recipes developed by the Murdoch Books Test Kitchen

©Text, design and illustrations Murdoch Books Pty Limited 2008. All rights reserved. No part of this publication may be reproduced, stored in a retrieval system or transmitted in any form or by any means, electronic, mechanical, photocopying, recording or otherwise without the prior written permission of the publisher.

National Library of Australia Cataloguing-in-Publication Data

Soups and breads. Includes index.
ISBN 9781921259074 (pbk.).
1. Soups. 2. Cookery (Bread). I. Price, Jane. (Series: Kitchen Classics; 9). 641.813
A catalogue record is available from the British Library.

Colour reproduction by Splitting Image Colour Studio, Melbourne, Australia
Printed by 1010 Printing International Limited in 2008. PRINTED IN CHINA.
Reprinted 2008.

IMPORTANT: Those who might be at risk from the effects of salmonella poisoning (the elderly, pregnant women, young children and those suffering from immune deficiency diseases) should consult their doctor with any concerns about eating raw eggs.

CONVERSION GUIDE: You may find cooking times vary depending on the oven you are using. For fan-forced ovens, as a general rule, set the oven temperature to 20°C (35°F) lower than indicated in the recipe. We have used 20 ml (4 teaspoon) tablespoon measures. If you are using a 15 ml (3 teaspoon) tablespoon, for most recipes the difference will not be noticeable. However, for recipes using baking powder, gelatine, bicarbonate of soda (baking soda), small amounts of flour, add an extra teaspoon for each tablespoon specified.

soups and breads

THE SOUP RECIPES YOU MUST HAVE

SERIES EDITOR **JANE PRICE**

MURDOCH BOOKS

CONTENTS

IN THE SOUP POT

Like the cleverest sort of quick-change artist, soup can be many different things depending upon the occasion. Some soups present as light, elegant entrées, raising the curtain on a stylish dinner party. Others are entire filling, meals-in-a-bowl, perfect for a casual family repast. Some soups are purée-smooth and silky, while others are composed of heartier ingredients and are as thick, chunky and rustic. Soup can be assembled from no more than the freshest of seasonal vegetables, perfect for those wanting low-fat meal ideas, or made indulgent with generous splashes of cream, coconut milk or the best quality olive oil. A soup can be the sort that takes hours to lovingly construct or the type that is whizzed together in a trice, just the thing for days when time is short. Soup can be summery and refreshing (like yoghurt soup or any tomato-based soup), or as warming and wintry as split pea and ham or roasted pumpkin soup. Soups come from all corners of the globe too so, depending on the mood, they can have the tang and spice of Asian flavours, be mellow with classic Mediterranean ingredients or soothe with the tastes and textures of homey favourites; think of chowder, minestrone or gumbo.

Whatever type of soup you choose to make, and whatever the occasion, one thing is for certain — absolutely nothing goes with soup better than bread. And the best bread for soup is always home-made. This can mean yeasty, slow-rise classics like crusty baguette, chewy ciabatta, golden bagels and baps, or more quickly constructed goodies like scones, popovers and muffins. The possibilities are endless! With bowls of steaming soup and morsels of crunchy bread at hand, a superbly delicious (not to mention nutritious and easy) meal, first course or snack is never that far away.

FRESH AND WHOLESOME

LENTIL AND SILVERBEET SOUP

CHICKEN STOCK

1 kg (2 lb 4 oz) chicken trimmings (necks, ribs, wings), fat removed

1 small onion, roughly chopped

1 bay leaf

3-4 flat-leaf (Italian) parsley sprigs

1-2 oregano or thyme sprigs

280 g (10 oz/1½ cups) brown lentils, washed

850 g (1 lb 14 oz) silverbeet (Swiss chard)

60 ml (2 fl oz/¼ cup) olive oil

1 large onion, finely chopped

4 garlic cloves, crushed

35 g (1¼ oz) finely chopped coriander (cilantro) leaves

80 ml (2½ fl oz/⅓ cup) lemon juice

lemon wedges, to serve

SERVES 6

To make the stock, put all the ingredients in a large saucepan, add 3 litres (105 fl oz/12 cups) water and bring to the boil. Skim off any scum from the surface. Reduce the heat and simmer for 2 hours. Strain the stock, discarding the chicken trimmings, onion and herbs. You will need 1 litre (35 fl oz/4 cups) of stock for the soup.

Skim any fat from the stock. Put the lentils in a large saucepan, then add the stock and 1 litre (35 fl oz/4 cups) water. Bring to the boil, then reduce the heat and simmer, covered, for 1 hour.

Meanwhile, remove the stems from the silverbeet and shred the leaves. Heat the oil in a saucepan over medium heat and cook the onion for 2-3 minutes, or until transparent. Add the garlic and cook for 1 minute. Add the silverbeet and toss for 2-3 minutes, or until wilted. Stir the mixture into the lentils. Add the coriander and lemon juice, season, and simmer, covered, for 15-20 minutes. Serve with the lemon wedges.

PREPARATION TIME: 20 MINUTES   COOKING TIME: 3 HOURS 30 MINUTES

NOTE: You can freeze any leftover stock for up to 3 months.

CARROT AND ORANGE SOUP

500 g (1 lb 2 oz) carrots, peeled
and sliced
30 g (1 oz) butter
125 ml (4 fl oz/½ cup) orange juice
1–1.25 litres (35–44 fl oz/4–5 cups)
vegetable stock
1 small onion, roughly chopped
3–4 teaspoons chopped thyme
sour cream, to serve
freshly grated nutmeg, to serve

SERVES 4

Put the carrots and butter in a large heavy-based saucepan and cook over medium heat for 10 minutes, stirring occasionally. Add the orange juice, vegetable stock and onion. Bring to the boil, add the thyme and season. Reduce the heat, cover and cook for 20 minutes, or until the carrots are tender. Allow to cool.

Process the mixture in a food processor or blender, in batches, until smooth. When ready to serve, return the mixture to the pan and reheat.

Spoon into individual bowls. Top each with a dollop of sour cream and sprinkle with nutmeg. Garnish with a small sprig of thyme, if desired.

PREPARATION TIME: 20 MINUTES   COOKING TIME: 35 MINUTES

FRENCH ONION SOUP

60 g (2¼ oz) butter
6 onions (about 1 kg/2 lb 4 oz), sliced into
fine rings
1 teaspoon sugar
3 tablespoons plain (all-purpose) flour
2.25 litres (79 fl oz/9 cups) vegetable
stock
1 baguette, cut into 1 cm (½ inch) slices
65 g (2½ oz/½ cup) grated gruyère or
cheddar cheese, plus extra, to serve

SERVES 4–6

Heat the butter in a large saucepan. Add the onion and cook slowly over low heat for about 20 minutes, or until tender. Add the sugar and flour and cook, stirring, for 1–2 minutes until the mixture is just starting to turn golden. Add the stock and bring to a simmer. Cover, and continue to cook over low heat for 1 hour, stirring occasionally. Season to taste.

Preheat the oven to 180°C (350°F/Gas 4). Bake the baguette slices for 20 minutes, turning once, until dry and golden. Top each slice with some of the grated cheese and place under a hot grill (broiler) until the cheese is melted. Serve the soup topped with the toasted cheese croutons. Sprinkle with extra grated cheese.

PREPARATION TIME: 20 MINUTES   COOKING TIME: 1 HOUR 45 MINUTES

SEAFOOD SOUP

4 tomatoes
500 g (1 lb 2 oz) raw prawns (shrimp)
1 tablespoon oil
5 cm (2 inch) piece fresh ginger, grated
3 tablespoons finely chopped lemon
grass (white part only)
3 small red chillies, finely chopped
2 onions, chopped
750 ml (26 fl oz/3 cups) fish stock
4 makrut (kaffir lime) leaves,
finely shredded
165 g (5¾ oz/1 cup) chopped pineapple
1 tablespoon tamarind concentrate
1 tablespoon grated palm sugar (jaggery)
or soft brown sugar
2 tablespoons lime juice
1 tablespoon fish sauce
500 g (1 lb 2 oz) skinless firm white fish
fillets, cut into 2 cm (¾ inch cubes)
2 tablespoons chopped coriander
(cilantro) leaves

SERVES 6

Score a cross in the base of the tomatoes. Put in a heatproof bowl and cover with boiling water. Leave for 30 seconds, then transfer to cold water and peel the skin away from the cross. Cut the tomatoes in half, scoop out the seeds and chop the flesh.

Peel the prawns and gently pull out the dark vein from each prawn back, starting from the head end.

Heat the oil in a large saucepan. Add the ginger, lemon grass, chilli and onion and stir over medium heat for 5 minutes or until the onion is golden.

Add the tomato to the pan and cook for 3 minutes. Stir in the fish stock, 750 ml (26 fl oz/3 cups) water, the lime leaves, pineapple, tamarind, palm sugar, lime juice and fish sauce. Cover, bring to the boil, then reduce the heat and simmer for 15 minutes.

Add the fish fillets, prawns and coriander to the pan, and simmer for 10 minutes or until the seafood is tender. Serve immediately.

PREPARATION TIME: 30 MINUTES   COOKING TIME: 40 MINUTES

FAST PASTA SOUP

1 tablespoon oil
2 spring onions (scallions), chopped
150 g (5½ oz) snow peas (mangetout), trimmed and cut into pieces
200 g (7 oz) mushrooms, sliced
2 garlic cloves, crushed
1 teaspoon grated fresh ginger
1 litre (35 fl oz/4 cups) vegetable stock
150 g (5½ oz) angel hair pasta

SERVES 4

Heat the oil in a saucepan over medium heat and stir-fry the spring onion, snow peas and mushrooms for a few minutes, or until just tender.

Add the garlic and grated fresh ginger and stir for a further minute. Pour in the vegetable stock and bring to the boil. Once boiling, add the pasta and cook for 3 minutes, or until just tender. Serve immediately.

PREPARATION TIME: 10 MINUTES   COOKING TIME: 10 MINUTES

MELOKHIA SOUP

1.25 litres (44 fl oz/5 cups) chicken stock
1 onion, halved
6 cracked cardamom pods
2 silverbeet (Swiss chard) leaves, finely chopped, stalks discarded
400 g (14 oz) packet frozen shredded melokhia leaves (see Note), or 30 g (1 oz) dried leaves, crumbled
2 tablespoons ghee
4 garlic cloves, crushed
1 teaspoon ground coriander
pinch chilli powder

DRESSING
1 small onion, finely chopped
2 tablespoons lemon juice

SERVES 4

Put the stock, onion and cardamom pods in a large saucepan, bring to the boil and boil for 12–15 minutes, or until the stock reduces to about 1 litre (35 fl oz/4 cups). Remove the onion and cardamom with a slotted spoon. Add the silverbeet and melokhia leaves to the pan. Bring to the boil, reduce the heat and simmer, uncovered, for 10 minutes.

Meanwhile, heat the ghee in a small saucepan and add the garlic and ¼ teaspoon salt. Cook over low heat, stirring constantly, until the garlic is golden. Remove from the heat and stir in the coriander and chilli.

To make the dressing, combine the ingredients in a small serving bowl. Set aside.

Stir the garlic mixture into the soup and simmer for 2 minutes. Serve with the dressing on the side.

PREPARATION TIME: 20 MINUTES   COOKING TIME: 35 MINUTES

NOTE: If you are using frozen cooked leaves, you will notice they appear to be mixed with egg white — don't try to rinse this off. Cooked melokhia leaves have a viscous consistency similar to okra and this is what gives the soup its characteristic texture.

CLEAR SOUP WITH SALMON QUENELLES

400 g (14 oz) salmon cutlets
1 litre (35 fl oz/4 cups) fish stock
125 ml (4 fl oz/½ cup) dry white wine
2 teaspoons lemon juice
1 small carrot, finely chopped
2 spring onions (scallions), sliced
2 dill sprigs
2 parsley sprigs
3 black peppercorns
1 egg white, chilled
ground white pepper, to taste
125 ml (4 fl oz/½ cup) pouring (whipping) cream, chilled
2 tablespoons chervil leaves

SERVES 4

Remove the skin and bones from the salmon and set aside. Weigh 150 g (5½ oz) of the fish, chop roughly, cover and chill.

To make the soup, combine the fish skin and bones in a large saucepan with the remaining salmon, fish stock, wine, lemon juice, carrot, spring onion, dill, parsley and peppercorns. Slowly bring to the boil, then reduce the heat, cover and simmer for 15 minutes. Strain the soup and discard the vegetables. (You won't be using the cooked salmon for this recipe, but you can use it as a sandwich filling. When cool, flake the salmon and mix with a little mayonnaise.)

Pour the soup into a clean saucepan, bring to the boil, then reduce the heat to just simmering. Season to taste.

To make the quenelles, process the reserved salmon in a food processor until finely chopped. Gradually add the egg white and process until very smooth. Transfer to a chilled bowl and season well with salt and ground white pepper. Whip the cream and quickly fold into the salmon. Shape quenelles using 2 teaspoons dipped in cold water. Add to the soup in two batches and poach for 2 minutes, or until cooked. Transfer the quenelles to warm soup bowls.

Heat the soup to almost boiling and carefully ladle over the quenelles. Sprinkle with chervil leaves and serve.

PREPARATION TIME: 20 MINUTES   COOKING TIME: 25 MINUTES

NOTES: Ocean trout can be used instead of salmon.
   To make light fluffy quenelles, the ingredients used should be almost ice cold. The mixture will make about 24 quenelles.

CHICKEN SOUP WITH VERMICELLI AND VEGETABLES

1 kg (2 lb 4 oz) chicken pieces (such as drumsticks and thighs)
6 spring onions (scallions), chopped
2 cm (³/₄ inch) piece fresh ginger, very finely sliced
2 bay leaves
4 tablespoons soy sauce
100 g (3½ oz) dried rice vermicelli
50 g (1³/₄ oz) spinach leaves, chopped
2 celery stalks, thinly sliced
200 g (7 oz) bean sprouts, trimmed
crisp fried onion, to garnish
chilli sauce, to serve

SERVES 4

Combine the chicken and 1.5 litres (52 fl oz/6 cups) water in a saucepan and bring to the boil. Skim off any scum. Add the spring onion, ginger, bay leaves, soy sauce and ¼ teaspoon each of salt and pepper, then reduce the heat and simmer for 30 minutes.

Put the vermicelli in a heatproof bowl. Cover it with boiling water and leave to soak for 10 minutes or until soft. Drain.

Arrange the vermicelli, spinach, celery and bean sprouts on a platter. To serve, each diner places a serving of vermicelli and a selection of vegetables in large individual serving bowls. Pour the chicken soup, including a couple of pieces of chicken, into each bowl. Sprinkle over the fried onion and season with chilli sauce.

PREPARATION TIME: 15 MINUTES   COOKING TIME: 45 MINUTES

CHICKEN PASTA SOUP

2 tablespoons olive oil
1 onion, finely diced
2 boneless, skinless chicken breasts, finely diced
90 g (3¼ oz) mushrooms, chopped
175 g (6 oz) spaghetti, broken into short lengths
1.5 litres (52 fl oz/6 cups) chicken stock
35 g (1¼ oz) torn basil leaves

SERVES 4

Heat the olive oil in a saucepan and cook the onion until soft and golden. Add the chicken, mushroom, spaghetti pieces and chicken stock. Bring to the boil.

Reduce the heat and simmer for 10 minutes. Stir in the basil leaves. Season to taste and serve immediately.

PREPARATION TIME: 20 MINUTES   COOKING TIME: 20 MINUTES

NOTE: This is quite a chunky soup. If you prefer a thinner style of soup, you can add more stock.

Chicken soup with vermicelli and vegetables

MEAT DUMPLING SOUP

1 tablespoon white sesame seeds
2 tablespoons oil
2 garlic cloves, finely chopped
150 g (5½ oz) lean minced (ground) pork
200 g (7 oz) lean minced (ground) beef
200 g (7 oz) Chinese cabbage (wong bok), finely shredded
100 g (3½ oz) bean sprouts, trimmed and chopped
100 g (3½ oz) mushrooms, finely chopped
3 spring onions (scallions), finely chopped
150 g (5½ oz) gow gee (egg) dumpling wrappers

SOUP
2.5 litres (87 fl oz/10 cups) beef stock
2 tablespoons soy sauce
3 cm (1¼ inch) piece fresh ginger, very finely sliced
4 spring onions (scallions), chopped, to serve

SERVES 4–6

To make the filling, toast the sesame seeds in a dry frying pan over medium heat for 3–4 minutes, shaking the pan gently, until the seeds are golden brown. Remove from the pan at once to prevent burning. Crush the seeds in a food mill or using a mortar and pestle.

Heat the oil in a saucepan. Cook the garlic and mince over medium heat until the meat changes colour, breaking up any lumps with a fork. Add the cabbage, sprouts, mushrooms and 80 ml (2½ fl oz/⅓ cup) water. Cook, stirring occasionally, for 5–6 minutes, or until the water evaporates and the vegetables soften. Add the spring onion, crushed sesame seeds and season to taste. Set aside.

Work with one gow gee wrapper at a time and keep the extra wrappers covered with a damp tea towel (dish towel). Place 1 teaspoon of filling on a wrapper, just off-centre, and gently smooth out the filling a little. Brush the edges of the wrapper with a little water and fold it over the filling to form a semi-circle. Press the edges together to seal. Repeat with the extra wrappers and filling.

To make the soup, combine the beef stock, soy sauce, ginger and half the spring onion in a large saucepan. Bring to the boil and simmer for 15 minutes.

Drop the dumplings into the soup and cook gently for 5 minutes, or until they change colour and look plump. Garnish with the remaining spring onion and serve immediately.

PREPARATION TIME: 45 MINUTES   COOKING TIME: 35 MINUTES

PAPPA AL POMODORO

750 g (1 lb 10 oz) vine-ripened tomatoes
1 loaf (about 450 g/1 lb) day-old crusty Italian bread
1 tablespoon olive oil
3 garlic cloves, crushed
1 tablespoon tomato paste (concentrated purée)
1.25 litres (44 fl oz/5 cups) hot vegetable stock or water
1 tablespoon torn basil leaves
2–3 tablespoons extra virgin olive oil, plus extra, to serve

SERVES 4

Score a cross in the base of the tomatoes. Put in a heatproof bowl and cover with boiling water. Leave for 30 seconds, then transfer to cold water and peel the skin away from the cross. Cut the tomatoes in half, scoop out the seeds and chop the flesh.

Discard most of the crust from the bread and tear the bread into 3 cm (1¼ inch) pieces.

Heat the oil in a large saucepan. Add the garlic, tomato and tomato paste, then reduce the heat and simmer, stirring occasionally, for 10–15 minutes, or until reduced. Add the stock and bring to the boil, stirring for about 3 minutes. Reduce the heat to medium, add the bread pieces and cook, stirring, for 5 minutes, or until the bread softens and absorbs most of the liquid. Add more stock or water if the soup is too thick. Remove from the heat.

Stir in the basil leaves and extra virgin olive oil, and leave for 5 minutes so the flavours have time to develop. Serve drizzled with a little extra virgin olive oil.

PREPARATION TIME: 25 MINUTES   COOKING TIME: 25 MINUTES

CHICKEN, LEEK AND CHICKPEA SOUP

1 litre (35 fl oz/4 cups) chicken stock
125 g (4½ oz) miniature pasta shapes
20 g (¾ oz) butter
1 leek, white part only, sliced
1 garlic clove, crushed
110 g (3¾ oz/½ cup) tinned chickpeas, drained and lightly roasted
1 tablespoon plain (all-purpose) flour
2 tablespoons finely chopped flat-leaf (Italian) parsley
pinch cayenne pepper
200 g (7 oz) chopped cooked chicken meat

SERVES 4

Bring the chicken stock to the boil in a large saucepan. Add the pasta to the stock and cook until just tender. Remove the pasta with a slotted spoon and set aside, keeping the stock on the heat and just boiling.

Meanwhile, melt the butter in a large saucepan, add the leek and garlic and stir until golden, but not brown. Add the chickpeas, toss for a minute and then sprinkle with the flour. Fry for about 10 seconds, then gradually blend in the boiling stock.

Add the parsley and cayenne pepper, and season to taste. Add the pasta and the chicken meat to the saucepan and bring back to the boil before serving in individual bowls.

PREPARATION TIME: 15 MINUTES   COOKING TIME: 20 MINUTES

Pappa al pomodoro

RED GAZPACHO

1 kg (2 lb 4 oz) vine-ripened tomatoes
2 slices day-old white Italian bread, crust removed, broken into pieces
1 red capsicum (pepper), seeded, membrane removed and roughly chopped
2 garlic cloves, chopped
1 small green chilli, chopped (optional)
1 teaspoon sugar
2 tablespoons red wine vinegar
2 tablespoons extra virgin olive oil
8 ice cubes

GARNISH
½ Lebanese (short) cucumber, seeded and finely diced
½ red capsicum (pepper), seeded, membrane removed and finely diced
½ green capsicum (pepper), seeded, membrane removed and finely diced
½ red onion, finely diced
½ ripe tomato, diced

SERVES 4

Score a cross in the base of the tomatoes. Put in a heatproof bowl and cover with boiling water. Leave for 30 seconds, then transfer to cold water and peel the skin away from the cross. Cut the tomatoes in half, scoop out the seeds and roughly chop.

Soak the bread in cold water for 5 minutes, then squeeze out any excess liquid. Put the bread in a food processor with the tomato, capsicum, garlic, chilli, sugar and vinegar, and process until combined and smooth.

With the motor running, add the oil to make a smooth creamy mixture. Season to taste. Refrigerate for at least 2 hours. Add a little extra vinegar, if desired.

To make the garnish, mix all the ingredients in a bowl. Put 2 ice cubes in each bowl of soup and serve the garnish in separate bowls.

PREPARATION TIME: 40 MINUTES +   COOKING TIME: NIL

GARLIC, PASTA AND FISH SOUP

80 ml (2½ fl oz/⅓ cup) olive oil
1 leek, white part only, trimmed and sliced
20–30 garlic cloves, thinly sliced
2 potatoes, chopped
2 litres (70 fl oz/8 cups) fish stock
70 g (2½ oz/½ cup) small pasta shapes
10 baby (pattypan) squash, halved
2 zucchini (courgettes), cut into thick slices
300 g (10½ oz) ling fillets, chopped into large pieces
1–2 tablespoons lemon juice
2 tablespoons shredded basil

SERVES 4–6

Heat the oil in a large saucepan, add the leek, garlic and potato and cook over medium heat for 10 minutes. Add 500 ml (17 fl oz/2 cups) of the stock and cook for 10 minutes. Allow to cool slightly before transferring to a food processor or blender and blending, in batches, until smooth.

Pour the remaining stock into the pan and bring to the boil. Add the pasta, squash and zucchini. Add the purée, and simmer for 15 minutes. When the pasta is soft, add the fish pieces and cook for 5 minutes, or until tender. Add the lemon juice and basil, and season to taste.

PREPARATION TIME: 30 MINUTES   COOKING TIME: 40 MINUTES

QUICK MISO SOUP

1 teaspoon dried wakame
2½ teaspoons instant dashi powder
1.5 litres (52 fl oz/6 cups) boiling water
125 ml (4 fl oz/½ cup) white miso paste
300 g (10½ oz) silken tofu, drained and cut into 1.5 cm (⅝ inch) cubes

SERVES 4

Soak the dried wakame in water for 10 minutes, or until tender. Drain.

Dissolve the dashi powder in the boiling water. Put the miso paste in a wok and add 80 ml (2½ fl oz/⅓ cup) dashi stock, stirring until smooth. Add the rest of the dashi stock and stir well.

Add the tofu to the stock with the wakame. Simmer until hot.

PREPARATION TIME: 15 MINUTES   COOKING TIME: 10 MINUTES

SHANGHAI CHICKEN AND NOODLE SOUP

2 litres (70 fl oz/8 cups) ready-made stock diluted with 500 ml (17 fl oz/2 cups) water

1 star anise

4 thin slices fresh ginger

600 g (1 lb 5 oz) boneless, skinless chicken breasts

375 g (13 oz) Shanghai noodles

200 g (7 oz) fresh asparagus, woody ends trimmed, cut into 3 cm (1¼ inch) pieces

1 tablespoon finely sliced fresh ginger

1½ tablespoons light soy sauce

1 tablespoon Chinese rice wine

½ teaspoon sugar

4 spring onions (scallions), thinly sliced on the diagonal

50 g (1¾ oz) watercress tips (optional)

¼ teaspoon sesame oil, to drizzle

soy sauce, extra, to serve (optional)

SERVES 4–6

Pour the stock into a non-stick wok and bring to the boil. Reduce to medium–low heat, add the star anise and ginger slices. Add the chicken and poach for 15–20 minutes, or until cooked through. Remove the chicken with a slotted spoon and set aside to cool. Leave the stock in the wok.

Meanwhile, bring 2 litres (70 fl oz/8 cups) water to the boil in a large saucepan and cook the noodles for 3 minutes. Drain and refresh under cold water.

Cut the chicken across the breast into 5 mm (¼ inch) slices. Return the stock to the boil and add the asparagus, ginger, soy sauce, rice wine, sugar and ½ teaspoon salt. Reduce the heat, add the noodles and simmer for 2 minutes. Return the chicken to the wok and cook for 1 minute, or until heated through.

Remove the noodles from the liquid with tongs and evenly divide among serving bowls. Divide the chicken, asparagus, spring onion and watercress (if using) among the bowls, then ladle the broth on top. Drizzle with sesame oil and serve with extra soy sauce, if desired.

PREPARATION TIME: 10 MINUTES   COOKING TIME: 35 MINUTES

CRAB AND CORN EGGFLOWER NOODLE BROTH

70 g (2½ oz) dried thin egg noodles
1 tablespoon peanut oil
1 teaspoon finely chopped fresh ginger
3 spring onions (scallions), thinly sliced, white and green parts separated
1.5 litres (52 fl oz/6 cups) chicken stock
80 ml (2½ fl oz/⅓ cup) mirin
250 g (9 oz) fresh baby corn, sliced on the diagonal into 1 cm (½ inch) slices
175 g (6 oz) fresh crabmeat
1 tablespoon cornflour (cornstarch) mixed with 1 tablespoon water
2 eggs, lightly beaten
2 teaspoons lime juice
1 tablespoon soy sauce
3 tablespoons torn coriander (cilantro) leaves

SERVES 4

Cook the noodles in a large saucepan of boiling salted water for 3 minutes, or until just tender. Drain, then rinse under cold water. Set aside.

Heat a non-stick wok over high heat, add the peanut oil and swirl to coat the side of the wok. Add the ginger and white part of the spring onion and cook over medium heat for 1–2 minutes. Add the stock, mirin and corn and bring to the boil, then simmer for 7 minutes. Stir in the noodles, crabmeat and cornflour mixture. Return to a simmer and stir constantly until it thickens. Reduce the heat and pour in the egg in a thin stream, stirring constantly — do not boil. Gently stir in the lime juice, soy sauce and half the coriander.

Divide the noodles among four bowls and ladle on the soup. Top with the green spring onion and remaining coriander leaves.

PREPARATION TIME: 15 MINUTES   COOKING TIME: 15 MINUTES

FAST RED LENTIL SOUP

1 tablespoon oil
1 onion, finely chopped
250 g (9 oz/1 cup) red lentils
425 g (15 oz) tinned crushed tomatoes
1 litre (35 fl oz/4 cups) vegetable stock
2 tablespoons chopped basil
sour cream, to serve

SERVES 4

Heat the oil in a saucepan over medium heat. Add the onion and fry for 2–3 minutes, or until soft.

Add the lentils, tomatoes and vegetable stock. Bring to the boil, then reduce the heat and simmer for 20 minutes. Stir in the chopped basil and serve topped with a small dollop of sour cream.

PREPARATION TIME: 5 MINUTES   COOKING TIME: 25 MINUTES

Crab and corn eggflower noodle broth

SPICY CHICKEN BROTH WITH CORIANDER PASTA

350 g (12 oz) chicken thighs or wings, skin removed
2 carrots, finely chopped
2 celery stalks, finely chopped
2 small leeks, white part only, finely chopped
3 egg whites
1.5 litres (52 fl oz/6 cups) chicken stock
Tabasco sauce

CORIANDER PASTA
60 g (2¼ oz/½ cup) plain (all-purpose) flour
1 egg
½ teaspoon sesame oil
90 g (3¼ oz) coriander (cilantro) leaves

SERVES 4

Put the chicken pieces, carrot, celery and leek in a large heavy-based saucepan. Push the chicken to one side and add the egg whites to the vegetables. Using a wire whisk, beat for a minute or so, until frothy (take care not to use a pan that can be scratched by the whisk).

Warm the stock in a separate saucepan, then gradually add the stock to the first pan, whisking continuously to froth the egg whites. Continue whisking while slowly bringing to the boil. Make a hole in the froth on top with a spoon and leave to simmer for 30 minutes, without stirring.

Line a large strainer with a damp tea towel (dish towel) or double thickness of muslin (cheesecloth) and strain the broth into a clean bowl (discard the chicken and vegetables). Season with salt, pepper and Tabasco sauce to taste. Set aside until you are ready to serve.

To make the coriander pasta, sift the flour into a bowl and make a well in the centre. Whisk the egg and oil together and pour into the well. Mix together to make a soft pasta dough and knead on a lightly floured surface for 2 minutes, until smooth.

Divide the pasta dough into four even portions. Roll one portion out very thinly and cover with a layer of evenly spaced coriander leaves. Roll out another portion of pasta and lay this on top of the leaves, then gently roll the layers together. Repeat with the remaining pasta and coriander.

Cut out squares of pasta around the leaves. The pasta may then be left to sit and dry out if it is not needed immediately. When you are ready to serve, heat the chicken broth gently in a pan. As the broth simmers, add the pasta and cook for 1 minute. Serve immediately.

PREPARATION TIME: 1 HOUR   COOKING TIME: 50 MINUTES

NOTE: The egg whites added to the vegetable and chicken stock make the broth very clear, rather than leaving it with the normal cloudy appearance of chicken stock. This is called clarifying the stock. When you strain the broth through a tea towel or muslin, don't press the solids to extract the extra liquid or the broth will become cloudy. It is necessary to make a hole in the froth on top to prevent the stock boiling over.

TOFU MISO SOUP

80 g (2³/4 oz/½ cup) dashi granules
100 g (3½ oz) miso paste
1 tablespoon mirin
250 g (9 oz) firm tofu, cubed
1 spring onion (scallion), sliced, to serve

SERVES 4

Using a wooden spoon, combine 1 litre (35 fl oz/4 cups) water and the dashi granules in a small saucepan and bring to the boil.

Combine the miso paste and mirin in a small bowl, then add to the pan. Stir the miso over medium heat, taking care not to let the mixture boil once the miso has dissolved, or it will lose flavour. Add the tofu cubes to the hot stock and heat, without boiling, over medium heat for 5 minutes. Serve in individual bowls, garnished with the spring onion.

PREPARATION TIME: 10 MINUTES   COOKING TIME: 15 MINUTES

CHINESE CHICKEN AND CORN SOUP

750 ml (26 fl oz/3 cups) chicken stock
2 x 200 g (7 oz) boneless, skinless chicken breasts
3-4 corn cobs
1 tablespoon vegetable oil
4 spring onions (scallions), thinly sliced, white and green parts separated
1 garlic clove, crushed
2 teaspoons grated fresh ginger
310 g (11 oz) tinned creamed corn
2 tablespoons light soy sauce
1 tablespoon Chinese rice wine
1 tablespoon cornflour (cornstarch)
2 teaspoons sesame oil

SERVES 4

Bring the stock to simmering point in a small saucepan. Add the chicken and remove the pan from the heat. Cover the pan and leave the chicken to cool in the liquid. Remove the chicken with a slotted spoon, then finely shred the meat using your fingers. Cut the corn kernels from the cobs — you should get about 400 g (14 oz/2 cups) of kernels.

Heat a wok over medium–high heat, add the oil and swirl to coat the side of the wok. Add the white part of the spring onion, garlic and ginger and stir-fry for 30 seconds. Add the stock, corn kernels, creamed corn, soy sauce, rice wine and 250 ml (9 fl oz/1 cup) water. Stir until the soup comes to the boil, then reduce the heat and simmer for 10 minutes. Add the chicken meat.

Meanwhile, stir the cornflour, sesame oil and 1 tablespoon water together in a small bowl until smooth. Add a little of the hot stock, stir together, then pour this mixture into the soup. Bring to simmering point, stirring constantly for 3-4 minutes, or until slightly thickened. Season to taste. Garnish with the spring onion greens.

PREPARATION TIME: 10 MINUTES   COOKING TIME: 15 MINUTES

SOUPE DE POISSON

1 large ripe tomato
1½ kg (3 lb 5 oz) chopped fish bones from
firm white fish
1 leek, white part only, chopped
1 carrot, chopped
1 celery stalk, chopped
1 garlic clove, chopped
1 bay leaf
3 parsley stalks
6 black peppercorns
250 ml (9 fl oz/1 cup) dry white wine
1 tablespoon lemon juice
250 g (9 oz) skinless firm white fish fillets
(such as snapper, perch, cod),
cut into bite-sized pieces
ground white pepper, to taste
2 tablespoons chervil leaves
¼ lemon, cut into very fine slices

SERVES 6

Score a cross in the base of the tomato. Put in a heatproof bowl and cover with boiling water. Leave for 30 seconds, then transfer to cold water and peel the skin away from the cross. Cut the tomato in half, scoop out the seeds and chop the flesh. Set aside.

Rinse the fish bones well in cold water and combine in a large saucepan with the leek, carrot, celery, garlic, bay leaf, parsley, peppercorns, wine, lemon juice and 2 litres (70 fl oz/8 cups) water. Slowly bring to the boil, skimming off any scum from the surface. Reduce the heat and simmer for 20 minutes.

Strain and discard the fish bones and vegetables. Strain the soup again, through a sieve lined with dampened muslin (cheesecloth), into a clean saucepan. Simmer, uncovered, for 10 minutes.

Add the fish pieces and simmer for 2 minutes, or until tender. Season to taste with salt and ground white pepper.

Divide the chopped tomato and chervil among six warm bowls and ladle the hot soup over them. Float some lemon slices on top and serve immediately.

PREPARATION TIME: 30 MINUTES   COOKING TIME: 45 MINUTES

NOTE: The straining muslin is dampened so it won't absorb too much of the cooking liquid.

BROCCOLI SOUP

2 tablespoons olive oil
1 large onion, thinly sliced
50 g (1¾ oz) diced prosciutto or unsmoked ham
1 garlic clove, crushed
1.25 litres (44 fl oz/5 cups) chicken stock
50 g (1¾ oz) stellini or other small pasta shapes
250 g (9 oz) broccoli, tops cut into small florets and the tender stems cut into thin batons
freshly grated parmesan cheese, to serve

SERVES 4

Heat the oil in a large saucepan over low heat, add the onion, prosciutto and garlic and cook for 4–5 minutes. Add the chicken stock, bring to the boil, reduce the heat slightly and simmer for 10 minutes with the lid three-quarters on.

Add the stellini and broccoli and cook until the pasta is *al dente* and the broccoli is crisp but tender. Season to taste. Serve in warm bowls with the grated parmesan.

PREPARATION TIME: 15 MINUTES   COOKING TIME: 20 MINUTES

COUNTRY PUMPKIN AND PASTA SOUP

1 tablespoon olive oil
30 g (1 oz) butter
1 large onion, finely chopped
2 garlic cloves, crushed
750 g (1 lb 10 oz) pumpkin (winter squash), cut into small cubes
2 potatoes, cut into small cubes
3 litres (105 fl oz/12 cups) vegetable stock
125 g (4½ oz) small pasta or risoni
1 tablespoon chopped parsley, (optional), to serve

SERVES 4–6

Heat oil and butter in a large saucepan. Add the onion and garlic and cook, stirring, for 5 minutes over low heat.

Add the pumpkin, potatoes and vegetable stock. Increase the heat, cover the pan and cook for 10 minutes, or until the vegetables are tender.

Add the pasta and cook, stirring occasionally, for 5 minutes, or until just tender. Serve immediately. Sprinkle with chopped parsley, if desired.

PREPARATION TIME: 25 MINUTES   COOKING TIME: 20 MINUTES

CAMBODIAN SOUR CHICKEN SOUP

800 g (1 lb 12 oz) chicken quarters (leg
and thigh), skin removed, cut into 5 cm
(2 inch) pieces on the bone
1 tablespoon tamarind pulp, soaked in
60 ml (2 fl oz/¼ cup) boiling water
60 ml (2 fl oz/¼ cup) fish sauce
½ teaspoon sugar
200 g (7 oz) fresh pineapple, cut into
2 cm (¾ inch) cubes
2 small tomatoes, cut into wedges
3 spring onions (scallions), finely chopped
1 teaspoon vegetable oil
4 garlic cloves, finely chopped
2 tablespoons chopped coriander
(cilantro) leaves
3 tablespoons chopped basil
1 red chilli, thinly sliced
2 tablespoons lime juice
90 g (3¼ oz/1 cup) bean sprouts, trimmed

SERVES 4

Pour 1.25 litres (44 fl oz/5 cups) water into a non-stick wok, then bring to the boil over medium heat. Add the chicken pieces and cook for 30 minutes, or until the stock is clear, occasionally skimming any scum from the surface. Remove the chicken from the wok with a slotted spoon, then take the meat off the bones and discard any fat and bones. Cool the meat slightly, then shred the chicken meat, keeping the stock simmering while you do this.

Strain the tamarind liquid to remove the seeds, then add the strained liquid to the stock. Return the shredded chicken meat to the wok, add the fish sauce, sugar, pineapple, tomato and spring onion and season to taste with salt, then cook for 1–2 minutes over medium heat, or until the chicken, tomato and pineapple are heated through.

Heat the oil in a small frying pan over medium heat and add the garlic. Cook for 2 minutes, or until golden. Remove the garlic with a slotted spoon and add it to the soup. Remove the wok from the heat and stir in the coriander, basil, chilli and lime juice. To serve, divide the bean sprouts in the bottom of four bowls and ladle the soup over the top. Serve immediately.

PREPARATION TIME: 20 MINUTES   COOKING TIME: 40 MINUTES

RICE SOUP WITH PRAWN AND EGG

12 raw prawns (shrimp)
3 teaspoons dashi granules
60 ml (2 fl oz/¼ cup) Shoyu (Japanese soy sauce)
2 tablespoons sake
1 tablespoon mirin
750 g (1 lb 10 oz/4 cups) cold cooked Japanese short-grain rice, rinsed well
3 eggs, beaten
2 teaspoons ginger juice (see Notes)
2 spring onions (scallions), finely chopped
mitsuba or shiso, to garnish (see Notes)

SERVES 4

Peel the prawns and gently pull out the dark vein from each prawn back, starting from the head end.

Dissolve the dashi granules in 1.5 litres (52 fl oz/6 cups) hot water, then combine with the Shoyu, sake, mirin and ½ teaspoon salt in a large saucepan and bring to the boil. Reduce the heat, then add the rice and simmer for 1 minute, or until heated through. Add the prawns and cook for a further 3 minutes, or until the prawns are pink and starting to curl.

Remove from the heat and drizzle the eggs over the top, place the lid on the pan and allow to sit for 1 minute before stirring the eggs through the soup along with the ginger juice and the spring onions. Season to taste, garnish with mitsuba or shiso if desired, and serve immediately as the eggs should not be allowed to set completely.

PREPARATION TIME: 15 MINUTES   COOKING TIME: 15 MINUTES

NOTES: Ginger juice is available in some health food stores.
Mitsuba is a Japanese herb that resembles flat-leaf (Italian) parsley. Shiso (also called perilla) is a member of the mint family.

SNOW PEA, PRAWN AND PASTA SOUP

12 raw king prawns (shrimp)
100 g (3½ oz) snow peas (mangetout), trimmed
1 tablespoon oil
2 onions, chopped
1.5 litres (52 fl oz/6 cups) chicken stock
½ teaspoon grated fresh ginger
200 g (7 oz) angel hair pasta or spaghettini
basil leaves, to garnish

SERVES 4

Peel the prawns, leaving the tails intact. Gently pull out the dark vein from each prawn back, starting from the head end. Slice any large snow peas into smaller pieces.

Heat the oil in a saucepan, add the onion and cook over low heat until soft. Add the chicken stock and bring to the boil. Add the fresh ginger, snow peas, prawns and pasta. Cook over medium heat for 4 minutes. Season to taste and serve immediately, garnished with fresh basil leaves.

PREPARATION TIME: 30 MINUTES   COOKING TIME: 15 MINUTES

Rice soup with prawn and egg

THAI SWEET AND SOUR CHICKEN SOUP

6 large dried red chillies

250 ml (9 fl oz/1 cup) boiling water

4 red Asian shallots, chopped

4 garlic cloves, chopped

2 tablespoons chopped fresh galangal

2 teaspoons chopped fresh turmeric

2 lemon grass stems, white part only, finely chopped

½ teaspoon grated lime zest

1 teaspoon shrimp paste

1 litre (35 fl oz/4 cups) chicken stock

6 makrut (kaffir lime) leaves

2 tablespoons tamarind purée

2 tablespoons fish sauce

30 g (1 oz/¼ cup) grated palm sugar (jaggery) or soft brown sugar

450 g (1 lb) boneless, skinless chicken breast, thinly sliced

200 g (7 oz) asparagus, woody ends trimmed and cut into thirds

100 g (3½ oz) baby corn, cut in half lengthways

200 g (7 oz) fresh pineapple, cut into 2 cm (¾ inch) cubes

SERVES 4–6

Soak the chillies in the boiling water for 20 minutes, then drain and chop. Put the chilli, shallot, garlic, galangal, turmeric, lemon grass, lime zest and shrimp paste in a food processor or blender and blend to a smooth paste, adding a little water if necessary.

Pour the stock and 250 ml (9 fl oz/1 cup) water into a non-stick wok, add the makrut leaves and bring to the boil over high heat. Stir in the blended chilli paste and simmer for 5 minutes. Add the tamarind, fish sauce, palm sugar, chicken (using your hands to separate the chicken slices), asparagus and baby corn and stir to prevent the chicken clumping. Simmer for 10 minutes, or until the chicken is cooked and the vegetables are tender. Stir in the pineapple before serving in individual bowls.

PREPARATION TIME: 20 MINUTES +   COOKING TIME: 20 MINUTES

NOTE: Use a non-stick or stainless steel wok for this recipe as the tamarind purée reacts with a regular wok and will taint the whole dish.

SCALLOPS WITH SOBA NOODLES AND DASHI BROTH

250 g (9 oz) dried soba noodles
60 ml (2 fl oz/¼ cup) mirin
60 ml (2 fl oz/¼ cup) light soy sauce
2 teaspoons rice vinegar
1 teaspoon dashi granules
2 spring onions (scallions), sliced
1 teaspoon finely chopped fresh ginger
24 large scallops (without roe)
5 fresh black fungus, chopped (see Note)
1 sheet nori, shredded

SERVES 4

Add the noodles to a large saucepan of boiling water and stir to separate. Return to the boil, adding 250 ml (9 fl oz/1 cup) cold water and repeat this step three times, as it comes to the boil. Drain and rinse under cold water.

Put the mirin, soy sauce, vinegar, dashi and 875 ml (30 fl oz/3½ cups) water in a non-stick wok. Bring to the boil, then reduce the heat and simmer for 3–4 minutes. Add the spring onion and ginger and keep at a gentle simmer.

Heat a chargrill pan or plate until very hot and sear the scallops in batches for 30 seconds each side. Remove from the pan. Divide the noodles and black fungus among four deep serving bowls. Pour 185 ml (6 fl oz/¾ cup) of the broth into each bowl and top with six scallops each. Garnish with the shredded nori and serve immediately.

PREPARATION TIME: 10 MINUTES   COOKING TIME: 15 MINUTES

NOTE: If fresh black fungus is not available, use dried and soak it in warm water for 20 minutes.

AJO BLANCO

1 loaf (200 g/7 oz) day-old white Italian bread
150 g (5½ oz/1 cup) whole blanched almonds
3–4 garlic cloves, chopped
125 ml (4 fl oz/½ cup) extra virgin olive oil
80 ml (2½ fl oz/⅓ cup) sherry or white wine vinegar
375 ml (13 oz/1½ cups) vegetable stock
2 tablespoons olive oil, extra
80 g (2¾ oz) day-old white Italian bread, extra, crust removed, cut into cubes
200 g (7 oz) small seedless green grapes

SERVES 4–6

Remove the crusts from the loaf of bread. Soak the bread in cold water for 5 minutes, then squeeze out any excess liquid. Chop the almonds and garlic in a processor until well ground. Add the bread and process until smooth.

With the motor running, add the oil in a slow steady stream until the mixture is the consistency of thick mayonnaise. Slowly add the sherry and 310 ml (10¾ fl oz/1¼ cups) of stock. Blend for 1 minute. Season with salt. Refrigerate for at least 2 hours. The soup thickens on refrigeration so you may need to add the remaining stock or water to thin it.

When ready to serve, heat the extra oil in a frying pan, add the bread cubes and toss over medium heat for 2–3 minutes, or until golden. Drain on paper towel. Serve the soup very cold. Garnish with bread cubes and grapes.

PREPARATION TIME: 20 MINUTES +   COOKING TIME: 3 MINUTES

Scallops with soba noodles and dashi broth

THAI LEMON GRASS BROTH WITH MUSSELS

1.5 kg (3 lb 5 oz) black mussels
1 tablespoon vegetable oil
5 spring onions (scallions), thinly sliced
2 garlic cloves, crushed
750 ml (26 fl oz/3 cups) chicken or fish stock
2½ tablespoons sliced fresh galangal or ginger
4 lemon grass stems, white part only, bruised
2 long red chillies, halved lengthways
6 makrut (kaffir lime) leaves, crushed
2 tablespoons roughly chopped coriander (cilantro) leaves

SERVES 4

Scrub the mussels with a stiff brush and pull out the hairy beards. Discard any broken mussels, or open ones that don't close when tapped on the bench. Rinse well.

Heat a wok over medium heat, add the oil and swirl to coat the side of the wok. Cook the spring onion and garlic for 1 minute, or until softened. Add the stock, galangal, lemon grass, chilli, makrut leaves and 750 ml (26 fl oz/3 cups) water and rapidly simmer for 15 minutes.

Add the mussels, cover with a lid, bring to the boil over high heat and cook for 7–8 minutes, or until the mussels open, tossing occasionally. Discard any unopened mussels.

Stir in half the coriander, then divide the broth and mussels among four large serving bowls. Sprinkle with the remaining coriander, then serve immediately.

PREPARATION TIME: 20 MINUTES   COOKING TIME: 25 MINUTES

SPINACH AND LENTIL SOUP

375 g (13 oz/2 cups) brown lentils
2 teaspoons olive oil
1 onion, finely chopped
2 garlic cloves, crushed
20 English spinach leaves, stalks removed,
leaves finely shredded
1 teaspoon ground cumin
1 teaspoon finely grated lemon zest
500 ml (17 fl oz/2 cups) vegetable stock
2 tablespoons finely chopped coriander
(cilantro)

SERVES 4–6

Put the lentils in a large saucepan with 1.25 litres (44 fl oz/5 cups) water. Bring to the boil and then simmer, uncovered, for 1 hour. Rinse and drain, then set aside.

In a separate saucepan heat the oil. Add the onion and garlic. Cook over medium heat until golden. Add the spinach and cook for a further 2 minutes.

Add the lentils, cumin, lemon zest, vegetable stock and 500 ml (17 fl oz/ 2 cups) water to the pan. Simmer, uncovered, for 15 minutes. Add the coriander and stir through. Serve immediately.

PREPARATION TIME: 10 MINUTES   COOKING TIME: 1 HOUR 25 MINUTES

KAKAVIA

2 onions, finely sliced
400 g (14 oz) tinned chopped tomatoes
750 g (1 lb 10 oz) potatoes, cut into 5 mm
(1/4 inch) slices
1 teaspoon chopped oregano
150 ml (5 fl oz) olive oil
2 litres (70 fl oz/8 cups) fish stock
1.5 kg (3 lb 5 oz) skinless, firm white fish
fillets (such as cod, jewfish or snapper),
cut into chunks
500 g (1 lb 2 oz) raw prawn (shrimp) meat
125 ml (4 fl oz/1/2 cup) lemon juice
chopped flat-leaf (Italian) parsley,
to garnish

SERVES 6

Layer the onion, tomato and potato in a large heavy-based saucepan, seasoning with salt, pepper and oregano between each layer.

Add the oil and stock and bring the mixture to the boil. Reduce the heat and simmer for 10 minutes, or until the potato is cooked through and tender.

Add the fish and prawn meat and cook for 5 minutes, or until the seafood is cooked. Add the lemon juice, spoon into bowls and top with parsley.

PREPARATION TIME: 20 MINUTES   COOKING TIME: 20 MINUTES

SCALLOP AND EGGFLOWER SOUP

300 g (10½ oz) scallops
1 tablespoon dry sherry
¼ teaspoon ground white pepper
1 teaspoon grated fresh ginger
7 spring onions (scallions), thinly sliced
white and green parts separated
2 tablespoons oil
1 tablespoon cornflour (cornstarch)
750 ml (26 fl oz/3 cups) chicken stock
2 tablespoons soy sauce
70 g (2½ oz) tinned straw mushrooms,
cut into halves
50 g (1¾ oz/⅓ cup) frozen peas
1 egg, lightly beaten
dry sherry, extra, to taste
2 teaspoons soy sauce, extra

SERVES 4

Slice or pull off any vein, membrane or hard white muscle from the scallops, leaving any roe attached. Combine with the sherry, pepper and ginger in a bowl and refrigerate for 10 minutes.

Heat the oil in a wok or heavy-based frying pan, swirling gently to coat the base and side. Add the white part of the spring onion and cook for 30 seconds. Add the scallops and their liquid and cook over high heat, turning occasionally, until the scallops turn milky white. Remove the scallops with a slotted spoon and set aside.

Blend the cornflour with a little of the stock until smooth, add to the wok with the remaining stock and soy sauce and bring to the boil, stirring until the mixture boils and thickens. Add the straw mushrooms and peas and cook for 2 minutes. Return the scallops to the wok, stirring the soup constantly.

Pour in the egg and cook, stirring until it turns opaque. Stir the spring onion greens through and add a little more sherry and soy sauce, to taste.

PREPARATION TIME: 30 MINUTES +   COOKING TIME: 45 MINUTES

NOTE: Drain and rinse straw mushrooms before using. Leftover tinned mushrooms can be kept chilled, covered with water, for up to 3 days. They can be used in dishes such as stir-fries.

LEMON-SCENTED BROTH WITH TORTELLINI

1 lemon
125 ml (4 fl oz/½ cup) white wine
440 g (15½ oz) tinned chicken consommé
375 g (13 oz) fresh or dried veal or chicken tortellini
4 tablespoons chopped flat-leaf (Italian) parsley

SERVES 4–6

Using a vegetable peeler, peel wide strips from the lemon. Remove the white pith with a small sharp knife. Cut three of the wide pieces into fine strips and set aside for garnishing.

Combine the remaining wide lemon strips, white wine, consommé and 750 ml (26 fl oz/3 cups) water in a large saucepan. Cook for 10 minutes over low heat. Remove the lemon zest from the pan and bring the mixture to the boil. Add the tortellini and parsley and season with black pepper. Cook for 6–7 minutes, or until the pasta is *al dente*. Garnish with fine strips of lemon zest.

PREPARATION TIME: 10 MINUTES   COOKING TIME: 20 MINUTES

WON TON SOUP

4 dried Chinese mushrooms
250 g (9 oz) raw prawns (shrimp)
250 g (9 oz) minced (ground) pork
1 tablespoon soy sauce
1 teaspoon sesame oil
2 spring onions (scallions), finely chopped
1 teaspoon grated fresh ginger
2 tablespoons tinned chopped water chestnuts
250 g (9 oz) packet won ton wrappers
cornflour (cornstarch), to dust
1.5 litres (52 fl oz/6 cups) chicken or beef stock
4 spring onions (scallions), extra, finely sliced, to garnish

SERVES 4–6

Soak the mushrooms in a bowl of hot water for 30 minutes. Drain, then squeeze to remove any excess liquid. Discard the stems and chop the caps finely. Peel the prawns and gently pull out the dark vein from each prawn back, starting at the head end. Finely chop the prawn meat and mix in a bowl with the mushrooms, pork, soy sauce, sesame oil, spring onion, ginger and water chestnuts.

Cover the won ton wrappers with a damp tea towel (dish towel) to prevent them drying out. Working with one wrapper at a time, place a heaped teaspoon of mixture on the centre of each. Moisten the pastry edges with water, fold in half diagonally and bring the two points together. Place on a tray dusted with cornflour until ready to cook.

Cook the won tons in a saucepan of rapidly boiling water for 4–5 minutes.

In a separate saucepan bring the stock to the boil. Remove the won tons with a slotted spoon and place in serving bowls. Scatter the spring onion over the top. Ladle the stock over the won tons.

PREPARATION TIME: 40 MINUTES +   COOKING TIME: 5 MINUTES

RED CAPSICUM SOUP

4 red capsicums (peppers)
4 tomatoes
60 ml (2 fl oz/¼ cup) oil
½ teaspoon dried marjoram
½ teaspoon dried mixed herbs
2 garlic cloves, crushed
1 teaspoon mild curry paste
1 red onion, sliced
1 leek, white part only, sliced
250 g (9 oz) green cabbage, chopped
1 teaspoon sweet chilli sauce

SERVES 6

Cut the capsicums into quarters. Remove the seeds and membrane. Grill (broil) until the skin blackens and blisters. Place on a cutting board, cover with a tea towel (dish towel) and allow to cool before peeling and chopping.

Score a cross in the base of the tomatoes. Put in a heatproof bowl and cover with boiling water. Leave for 30 seconds, then transfer to cold water and peel the skin away from the cross. Cut the tomatoes in half, scoop out the seeds and chop the flesh.

Heat the oil in a large saucepan. Add the herbs, garlic and curry paste. Stir over low heat for 1 minute, or until aromatic. Add the onion and leek and cook for 3 minutes or until golden. Add the cabbage, capsicum, tomato and 1 litre (35 fl oz/4 cups) water. Bring to the boil, reduce heat and simmer for 20 minutes. Remove from the heat.

Allow to cool slightly before transferring to a food processor and blending, in batches, for 30 seconds, or until smooth. Return the soup to a clean saucepan, stir through the chilli sauce and season to taste with salt and freshly ground black pepper. Reheat gently and serve hot.

PREPARATION TIME: 20 MINUTES   COOKING TIME: 30 MINUTES

TOM YUM GOONG

500 g (1 lb 2 oz) raw prawns (shrimp)
1 tablespoon oil
2 tablespoons red curry paste
2 tablespoons tamarind concentrate
2 teaspoons ground turmeric
1 teaspoon chopped red chilli (optional)
4-8 makrut (kaffir lime) leaves, shredded
2 tablespoons fish sauce
2 tablespoons lime juice
2 teaspoons soft brown sugar
10 g (¼ oz) coriander (cilantro) leaves

SERVES 4–6

Peel the prawns, leaving the tails intact and reserving the shells and heads. Gently pull out the dark vein from each prawn back, starting at the head end.

Heat the oil in a large saucepan, add the prawn shells and heads to the pan and cook for 10 minutes over high heat, tossing frequently, until the shells and heads are deep orange in colour.

Have 2 litres (70 fl oz/8 cups) water ready. Add 250 ml (9 fl oz/1 cup) of the water and the curry paste to the pan. Boil for 5 minutes, until liquid is reduced slightly. Add the remaining water and simmer for 20 minutes. Drain the stock, discarding the prawn heads and shells.

Return the drained stock to the pan. Add the tamarind concentrate, turmeric, chilli and makrut leaves, bring to the boil and cook for 2 minutes. Add the prawns to the pan and cook for 5 minutes or until the prawns turn pink. Add the fish sauce, lime juice and sugar and stir to combine. Serve immediately, sprinkled with coriander leaves.

PREPARATION TIME: 25 MINUTES   COOKING TIME: 45 MINUTES

TORTELLINI BROTH

250 g (9 oz) tortellini
1 litre (35 fl oz/4 cups) beef stock
30 g (1 oz/½ cup) sliced spring onions
(scallions), plus extra, for garnish

SERVES 4

Cook the tortellini in a large saucepan of rapidly boiling salted water until *al dente*. Drain and divide among four deep soup bowls.

While the tortellini is cooking, bring the beef stock to the boil in a separate saucepan. Add the spring onion and simmer for 3 minutes. Ladle the stock over the tortellini and garnish with the extra spring onion.

PREPARATION TIME: 5 MINUTES   COOKING TIME: 10 MINUTES

Tom yum goong

RICH AND CREAMY

MARMITE DIEPPOISE

500 g (1 lb 2 oz) raw prawns (shrimp)
600 g (1 lb 5 oz) black mussels
350 g (12 oz) scallops
300 g (10½ oz) assorted skinless firm white fish fillets (such as monkfish, snapper, orange roughy, salmon)
½ leek, white part only, sliced
½ small fennel bulb, sliced
375 ml (13 fl oz/1½ cups) dry white wine
2 thyme sprigs
1 bay leaf
150 g (5½ oz) button mushrooms, sliced
250 ml (9 fl oz/1 cup) pouring (whipping) cream
1 tablespoon chopped flat-leaf (Italian) parsley

SERVES 4

Peel the prawns and gently pull out the dark vein from each prawn back, starting at the head end. Scrub the mussels with a stiff brush and pull out the hairy beards. Discard any broken mussels, or open ones that don't close when tapped on the bench. Rinse well. Slice or pull off any vein, membrane or hard white muscle from the scallops, leaving any roe attached. Cut the fish fillets into bite-sized cubes.

In a large heavy-based saucepan, combine the leek, fennel, wine, thyme, bay leaf and mussels. Bring to the boil, cover and simmer for 4–5 minutes, stirring occasionally, until the mussels are cooked. Remove the mussels from the pan with tongs, discarding any unopened ones. Remove the mussels from their shells and discard the shells. Set aside.

Bring the cooking liquid to simmering point. Add the prawns and scallops, cover and simmer for 2 minutes, or until cooked. Remove the prawns and scallops and set aside.

Return the cooking liquid to simmering point and add the fish. Poach for 3 minutes, or until cooked, then remove the fish and set aside. Line a sieve with a double layer of dampened muslin (cheesecloth) and strain the liquid into a clean saucepan. Bring to the boil, add the mushrooms and cook, uncovered, over high heat for 3 minutes. Stir in the cream, bring to the boil and simmer for about 5 minutes, stirring occasionally, until thick enough to coat the back of a spoon.

Return the mussels, prawns, scallops and fish to the stock and simmer until heated through. Season, stir in the parsley and serve.

PREPARATION TIME: 45 MINUTES   COOKING TIME: 30 MINUTES

TOM KHA GAI

5 cm (2 inch) piece fresh galangal,
thinly sliced
500 ml (17 fl oz/2 cups) coconut milk
250 ml (9 fl oz/1 cup) chicken stock
600 g (1 lb 5 oz) boneless, skinless
chicken breasts, cut into thin strips
1–2 teaspoons finely chopped red chilli
2 tablespoons fish sauce
1 teaspoon soft brown sugar
10 g (1/4 oz) coriander (cilantro) leaves
coriander (cilantro) sprigs, to garnish

SERVES 4

Combine the galangal, coconut milk and chicken stock in a saucepan. Bring to the boil, then reduce the heat and simmer over low heat for 10 minutes, stirring occasionally. Add the chicken and chilli to the pan and simmer for 8 minutes. Add the fish sauce and sugar and stir to combine. Add the coriander leaves and serve immediately, garnished with coriander sprigs.

PREPARATION TIME: 20 MINUTES   COOKING TIME: 20 MINUTES

YOGHURT SOUP

1.5 litres (52 fl oz/6 cups) vegetable stock
70 g (2 1/2 oz/1/3 cup) short-grain white rice
80 g (2 3/4 oz) butter
50 g (1 3/4 oz) plain (all-purpose) flour
250 g (9 oz/1 cup) plain yoghurt
1 egg yolk
1 tablespoon finely sliced mint leaves
1/4 teaspoon cayenne pepper

SERVES 4–6

Put the stock and rice in a saucepan and bring to the boil over high heat. Reduce the heat to medium-low and simmer for 10 minutes, then remove from heat and set aside.

In another saucepan, melt 60 g (2 1/4 oz) of the butter over low heat. Stir in the flour and cook for 2–3 minutes, or until pale and foaming. Gradually add the stock and rice mixture, stirring constantly, and cook over medium heat for 2 minutes, or until the mixture thickens slightly. Reduce the heat to low.

In a small bowl, whisk together the yoghurt and egg yolk, then gradually pour into the soup, stirring constantly. Remove from the heat and stir in the mint and 1/2 teaspoon salt.

Just before serving, melt the remaining butter in a small saucepan over medium heat. Add the cayenne pepper and cook until the mixture is lightly browned. Pour over the soup.

PREPARATION TIME: 15 MINUTES   COOKING TIME: 20 MINUTES

CREAMY RED LENTIL SOUP

CROUTONS
4 thick bread slices, crusts removed
60 g (2¼ oz) butter
1 tablespoon oil

1½ teaspoons cumin seeds
80 g (2¾ oz) butter
1 large brown onion, diced
185 g (6½ oz/¾ cup) red lentils, rinsed and drained
1.5 litres (52 fl oz/6 cups) vegetable stock
2 tablespoons plain (all-purpose) flour
2 egg yolks
185 ml (6 fl oz/¾ cup) milk

SERVES 6

To make the croutons, cut the bread into 1 cm (½ inch) cubes. Heat the butter and oil in a frying pan and when the butter foams, add the bread and cook over medium heat until golden and crisp. Drain on crumpled paper towel.

In a small frying pan, dry roast the cumin seeds until they start to pop and become aromatic. Leave to cool, then grind to a fine powder using a mortar and pestle.

Melt half the butter in a heavy-based saucepan and cook the onion over medium heat for 5–6 minutes, until softened. Add the lentils, cumin and stock and bring to the boil. Cover and simmer for 30–35 minutes, until the lentils are very soft. Allow to cool slightly before transferring to a food processor and blending, in batches, until smooth.

In a large heavy-based saucepan, melt the remaining butter over low heat. Stir in the flour and cook for 2–3 minutes, or until pale and foaming. Stirring constantly, add the lentil purée gradually, then simmer for 4–5 minutes.

In a small bowl, combine the egg yolks and milk. Whisk a small amount of the soup into the egg mixture and then return it all to the soup, stirring constantly. Be careful not to boil the soup or the egg will curdle. Season to taste. Heat the soup to just under boiling and serve with the croutons.

PREPARATION TIME: 25 MINUTES   COOKING TIME: 1 HOUR

PUMPKIN, PRAWN AND COCONUT SOUP

500 g (1 lb 2 oz) pumpkin (winter squash), diced
80 ml (2½ fl oz/⅓ cup) lime juice
1 kg (2 lb 4 oz) raw large prawns (shrimp)
2 onions, chopped
1 small fresh red chilli, finely chopped
1 lemon grass stem, white part only, chopped
1 teaspoon shrimp paste
1 teaspoon sugar
375 ml (13 fl oz/1½ cups) coconut milk
1 teaspoon tamarind purée
125 ml (4 fl oz/½ cup) coconut cream
1 tablespoon fish sauce
2 tablespoons Thai basil leaves, plus extra, to serve

SERVES 4–6

Combine the pumpkin with half the lime juice in a bowl. Peel the prawns and gently pull out the dark vein from each prawn back, starting at the head end.

Process the onion, chilli, lemon grass, shrimp paste, sugar and 60 ml (2 fl oz/¼ cup) coconut milk in a food processor until a paste forms.

Combine the paste with the remaining coconut milk, tamarind purée and 250 ml (9 fl oz/1 cup) water in a large saucepan and stir until smooth. Add the pumpkin and lime juice to the pan and bring to the boil. Reduce the heat and simmer, covered, for about 10 minutes, or until the pumpkin is just tender.

Add the prawns and coconut cream, then simmer for 3 minutes, or until the prawns are just pink and cooked through. Stir in the fish sauce, the remaining lime juice and the Thai basil leaves.

To serve, pour the soup into warmed bowls and garnish with basil leaves.

PREPARATION TIME: 15 MINUTES   COOKING TIME: 20 MINUTES

AVGOLEMONO SOUP WITH CHICKEN

1 onion, halved

2 whole cloves

1 carrot, cut into chunks

1 bay leaf

500 g (1 lb 2 oz) boneless, skinless chicken breast

70 g (2½ oz/⅓ cup) short-grain rice

3 eggs, separated

60 ml (2 fl oz/¼ cup) lemon juice

2 tablespoons chopped flat-leaf (Italian) parsley

4 thin lemon slices, to garnish

SERVES 4

Stud the onion with the cloves and place in a large saucepan with 1.5 litres (52 fl oz/6 cups) water. Add the carrot, bay leaf and chicken and season. Slowly bring to the boil, then reduce the heat and simmer for 10 minutes, or until the chicken is cooked.

Strain the stock into a clean saucepan, reserving the chicken and discarding the vegetables. Add the rice to the stock, bring to the boil, then reduce the heat and simmer for 15 minutes, or until the rice is tender. Meanwhile, tear the chicken into shreds.

Whisk the egg whites in a clean dry bowl until stiff peaks form, then beat in the yolks. Slowly beat in the lemon juice. Gently stir in about 170 ml (5½ fl oz/⅔ cup) of the hot (not boiling) stock and beat thoroughly. Add the egg mixture to the stock and heat gently, but do not let it boil, otherwise the eggs may scramble. Add the chicken and season to taste.

Set aside for 2–3 minutes to allow the flavours to develop. To serve spoon into bowls, sprinkle with parsley and garnish with lemon slices.

PREPARATION TIME: 20 MINUTES   COOKING TIME: 30 MINUTES

CREAMY FISH SOUP

¼ teaspoon saffron threads
2 tablespoons boiling water
1 litre (35 fl oz/4 cups) fish stock
125 ml (4 fl oz/½ cup) dry white wine
1 onion, finely chopped
1 small carrot, finely chopped
1 celery stalk, chopped
1 bay leaf
50 g (1¾ oz) butter
2 tablespoons plain (all-purpose) flour
300 g (10½ oz) skinless firm white fish fillets (such as snapper, orange roughy, bream), cut into bite-sized pieces
250 ml (9 fl oz/1 cup) pouring (whipping) cream
2 teaspoons snipped chives, to garnish

SERVES 4–6

In a small bowl, soak the saffron threads in the boiling water.

Put the fish stock, wine, onion, carrot, celery and bay leaf in a large saucepan and slowly bring to the boil. Cover and simmer for 20 minutes. Strain and discard the vegetables. Stir the saffron (with the liquid) into the hot stock.

In a clean saucepan, melt the butter and stir in the flour for 2 minutes, or until pale and foaming. Remove from the heat and gradually stir in the fish stock. Return to the heat and stir until the mixture boils and thickens. Add the fish and simmer for 2 minutes, or until the fish is cooked. Stir in the cream and heat through without boiling. Season to taste. Serve garnished with the chives.

PREPARATION TIME: 10 MINUTES   COOKING TIME: 35 MINUTES

CREAM OF OYSTER SOUP

18 fresh oysters, on the half shell
15 g (½ oz) butter
1 small onion, finely chopped
125 ml (4 fl oz/½ cup) white wine
375 ml (13 fl oz/1½ cups) fish stock
250 ml (9 fl oz/1 cup) pouring (whipping) cream
6 whole black peppercorns
6 basil leaves, torn
1 teaspoon lime juice
spring onions (scallions), shredded, to garnish
basil leaves, extra, shredded, to garnish

SERVES 4

Drain the oysters in a small strainer and reserve the juice and oysters separately. Roughly chop six of the oysters. Melt the butter in a small saucepan and add the onion. Cover and cook over low heat until soft but not brown, stirring occasionally. Add the wine and simmer for 5 minutes, or until reduced by half.

Add the stock to the pan, simmer for 2 minutes, then add the cream, peppercorns, basil and chopped oysters and simmer for 5 minutes. Strain, then push the mixture against the sides of the strainer, to extract as much flavour as possible. Discard the solids in the strainer.

Return the liquid to the pan and bring to the boil. Add the lime juice and reserved oyster juice. Season to taste. Spoon into four small bowls and add three oysters to each. Top with cracked black pepper. Garnish with spring onion and basil.

PREPARATION TIME: 15 MINUTES   COOKING TIME: 20 MINUTES

CHICKEN MULLIGATAWNY

STOCK

1.5 kg (3 lb 5 oz) chicken
1 carrot, chopped
2 celery stalks, chopped
4 spring onions (scallions), chopped
2 cm (3/4 inch) piece of fresh ginger, sliced

2 tomatoes, peeled
20 g (3/4 oz) ghee
1 large onion, finely chopped
3 garlic cloves, crushed
8 curry leaves
55 g (2 oz/1/4 cup) Madras curry paste
250 g (9 oz/1 cup) red lentils, washed and drained
70 g (2½ oz/1/3 cup) short-grain rice
250 ml (9 fl oz/1 cup) coconut cream
2 tablespoons coriander (cilantro) leaves, chopped
mango chutney, to serve

SERVES 6

To make the stock, put all the ingredients and 4 litres (140 fl oz/16 cups) cold water in a large stockpot or saucepan. Bring to the boil, removing any scum that rises to the surface. Reduce the heat to low and simmer, partly covered, for 3 hours. Continue to remove any scum from the surface. Carefully remove the chicken and cool. Strain the stock into a bowl and cool. Cover and refrigerate overnight. Discard the skin and bones from the chicken and shred the flesh into small pieces. Cover and refrigerate overnight.

Score a cross in the base of the tomatoes. Put in a heatproof bowl and cover with boiling water. Leave for 30 seconds then transfer to a bowl of cold water and peel the skin away from the cross. Cut the tomatoes in half, scoop out the seeds and chop the flesh.

Melt the ghee in a large saucepan over medium heat. Cook the onion for 5 minutes, or until softened but not browned. Add the garlic and curry leaves and cook for 1 minute. Add the curry paste, cook for 1 minute, then stir in the lentils. Pour in the stock and bring to the boil over high heat, removing any scum from the surface. Reduce the heat, add the tomato and simmer for 30 minutes, or until the lentils are soft.

Meanwhile, bring a large saucepan of water to the boil. Add the rice and cook for 12 minutes, stirring once or twice. Drain. Stir the rice into the soup with the chicken and coconut cream until warmed through — don't allow it to boil or it will curdle. Season. Sprinkle with the coriander and serve with the mango chutney.

PREPARATION TIME: 25 MINUTES +   COOKING TIME: 4 HOURS

CARROT AND CORIANDER SOUP

2 tablespoons olive oil
1 onion, chopped
800 g (1 lb 12 oz) carrots, roughly chopped
1 bay leaf
1 teaspoon ground cumin
1 teaspoon cayenne pepper
1 teaspoon ground coriander
2 teaspoons paprika
1.25 litres (44 fl oz/5 cups) chicken or vegetable stock
250 g (9 oz/1 cup) Greek-style yoghurt
2 tablespoons chopped coriander (cilantro) leaves
coriander (cilantro) leaves, extra, to garnish

SERVES 4

Heat the olive oil in a saucepan, add the onion and carrot and cook over low heat for 30 minutes. Add the bay leaf and spices and cook for a further 2 minutes. Add the stock, bring to the boil, then reduce the heat and simmer, uncovered, for 40 minutes, or until the carrot is tender. Allow to cool slightly, before transferring to a food processor and blending, in batches, until smooth. Return to a clean saucepan and gently reheat. Season to taste.

Combine the yoghurt and coriander in a bowl. Pour the soup into bowls and serve with a dollop of the yoghurt mixture. Garnish with coriander.

PREPARATION TIME: 15 MINUTES   COOKING TIME: 1 HOUR 10 MINUTES

FAST MUSHROOM SOUP

60 g (2¼ oz) butter
2 onions, chopped
500 g (1 lb 2 oz) button mushrooms, chopped
30 g (1 oz/¼ cup) plain (all-purpose) flour
500 ml (17 fl oz/2 cups) milk
375 ml (13 fl oz/1½ cups) vegetable stock
sour cream, to serve
chopped flat-leaf (Italian) parsley, to serve

SERVES 4

Heat the butter in a saucepan and fry the onions for 5 minutes, or until they are lightly golden. Add the mushrooms and cook for a further 5 minutes, stirring often. Add the flour and stir for 1 minute. Stir in the milk and vegetable stock. Reduce the heat and simmer, uncovered, for 10–15 minutes, or until the soup has thickened and the mushrooms are tender.

Serve in bowls, topped with a dollop of sour cream and parsley.

PREPARATION TIME: 5 MINUTES   COOKING TIME: 25 MINUTES

Carrot and coriander soup

BOURRIDE

1 tablespoon butter
1 tablespoon olive oil
4 slices white bread, crusts removed and cut into 1.5 cm (5/8 inch) cubes
2 kg (4 lb 8 oz) assorted firm white fish fillets (such as bass, whiting and cod)
5 egg yolks
4 garlic cloves, crushed
3–5 teaspoons lemon juice
250 ml (9 fl oz/1 cup) olive oil

STOCK
80 ml (2½ fl oz/⅓ cup) olive oil
1 large onion, chopped
1 carrot, sliced
1 leek, white part only, chopped
420 ml (14½ fl oz/1⅔ cups) dry white wine
1 teaspoon dried fennel seeds
2 garlic cloves, bruised
2 bay leaves
1 large strip orange zest
2 thyme sprigs

SERVES 8

To make the croutons, heat the butter and oil in a heavy-based frying pan. When the butter begins to foam, add the bread cubes and cook for 5 minutes, or until golden. Drain on crumpled paper towel. Set aside.

Fillet the fish (or ask your fishmonger to do it), reserving the heads and bones for the stock.

To make the aïoli, put 2 of the egg yolks, garlic and 3 teaspoons lemon juice in a food processor and blend until creamy. With the motor still running, slowly drizzle in the oil. Season and add the remaining lemon juice, to taste. Set aside until needed.

To make the stock, heat the olive oil in large saucepan or stockpot and add the onion, carrot and leek. Cook over low heat for 12–15 minutes, or until the vegetables are soft. Add the fish heads and bones, wine, fennel seed, garlic, bay leaves, orange zest, thyme, black pepper and ½ teaspoon salt. Cover with 2 litres (70 fl oz/8 cups) water. Bring to the boil and skim off the froth. Reduce the heat and simmer for 30 minutes. Strain into a pot, crushing the bones well to release as much flavour as possible. Return to the heat.

Preheat the oven to 120°C (235°F/Gas ½). Cut the fish fillets into large pieces about 9 cm (3½ inches) long. Add to the stock and bring to a simmer, putting the heavier pieces in first and adding the more delicate pieces later. Poach for 6–8 minutes, until the flesh starts to become translucent and begins to flake easily. Transfer the fish pieces to a serving platter and moisten with a little stock. Cover with foil and keep warm in the oven.

Place 8 tablespoons of the aïoli in a large bowl and slowly add the remaining 3 egg yolks, stirring constantly. Ladle a little stock into the aïoli mixture, blend well and return slowly to the rest of the stock. Stir continuously with a wooden spoon for 8–10 minutes over low heat, or until the soup has thickened and coats the back of a spoon. Do not boil or the mixture will curdle.

To serve, scatter the croutons and fish pieces into individual bowls and ladle the stock over the top.

PREPARATION TIME: 25 MINUTES   COOKING TIME: 1 HOUR 10 MINUTES

WILD RICE SOUP

95 g (3¼ oz/½ cup) wild rice
1 tablespoon oil
1 onion, finely chopped
2 celery stalks, finely chopped
1 green capsicum (pepper), seeded,
membrane removed and finely chopped
4 back bacon slices, finely chopped
4 open cap mushrooms, thinly sliced
1 litre (35 fl oz/4 cups) chicken stock
125 ml (4 fl oz/½ cup) pouring (whipping)
cream
1 tablespoon finely chopped flat-leaf
(Italian) parsley

SERVES 6

Put the wild rice in a saucepan with 500 ml (17 fl oz/2 cups) water and bring to the boil. Cook for 40 minutes, or until the rice is tender. Drain and rinse well.

Heat the oil in a large saucepan and add the onion, celery, capsicum and bacon. Fry for 8 minutes, or until the onion has softened and the bacon has browned. Add the mushrooms and cook for 1–2 minutes. Pour in the chicken stock and bring to the boil, then add the rice, stir, and cook the mixture for 2 minutes. Remove from the heat.

Stir in the cream and parsley, then reheat until the soup is almost boiling. Serve in deep bowls.

PREPARATION TIME: 15 MINUTES   COOKING TIME: 1 HOUR

WATERCRESS SOUP

100 g (3½ oz) butter
1 onion, roughly chopped
4 spring onions (scallions), roughly
chopped
450 g (1 lb) watercress, trimmed and
roughly chopped
40 g (1½ oz/⅓ cup) plain (all-purpose)
flour
750 ml (26 fl oz/3 cups) vegetable stock
sour cream or pouring (whipping) cream,
to serve

SERVES 4–6

Heat the butter in a large saucepan and add the onion, spring onion and watercress. Stir over low heat for 3 minutes, or until the vegetables have softened. Add the flour and stir until combined. Gradually add the stock and 310 ml (10¾ fl oz/1¼ cups) water. Stir until smooth and the mixture boils and thickens. Simmer, covered, over low heat for 10 minutes, or until the watercress is tender.

Allow to cool slightly and transfer the mixture to a food processor and process, in batches, until smooth. Before serving, gently heat through and season to taste. Serve with a dollop of sour cream or cream.

PREPARATION TIME: 15 MINUTES   COOKING TIME: 15–20 MINUTES

Wild rice soup

CREAMY MUSSEL SOUP

750 g (1 lb 10 oz) black mussels
1 celery stalk, chopped
1 carrot, chopped
1 onion, chopped
10 black peppercorns
4 flat-leaf (Italian) parsley stalks
100 g (3½ oz) butter, softened
3 spring onions (scallions), chopped
2 garlic cloves, crushed
1 large potato, cut into small cubes
185 ml (6 fl oz/¾ cup) white wine
40 g (1½ oz/⅓ cup) plain (all-purpose) flour
250 ml (9 fl oz/1 cup) pouring (whipping) cream
2 tablespoons chopped flat-leaf (Italian) parsley

SERVES 4

Scrub the mussels with a stiff brush and pull out the hairy beards. Discard any broken mussels or open ones that don't close when tapped on the bench. Rinse well. Put the mussels in a large saucepan with the celery, carrot, onion, peppercorns, parsley and 1.5 litres (52 fl oz/ 6 cups) water. Bring to the boil, reduce the heat and simmer, covered, for 4–5 minutes.

Strain the stock through a fine sieve and discard any unopened mussels. Remove the meat from the remaining mussels and set aside. Discard the shells and vegetables. Return the stock to the pan and simmer for 15 minutes. Remove from the heat. Set aside.

Melt half the butter in a large saucepan, add the spring onion, garlic and potato and stir over medium heat for 3 minutes, or until the onion is soft. Add the wine and bring to the boil. Reduce the heat and simmer for 1 minute.

Blend the flour and remaining butter in a bowl to form a paste. Pour 875 ml (30 fl oz/3½ cups) of the stock into the saucepan with the garlic and potato. Gradually add the butter mixture, whisking until the mixture boils and thickens. Reduce the heat and simmer for 15 minutes, or until the potato is cooked. Stir in the mussel meat and cream until heated through. Stir in the parsley just before serving.

PREPARATION TIME: 30 MINUTES   COOKING TIME: 40 MINUTES

THAI PUMPKIN AND COCONUT SOUP

250 g (9 oz) small raw prawns (shrimp)
½ teaspoon shrimp paste
2 long red chillies, chopped
¼ teaspoon white peppercorns
2 tablespoons chilli paste
2 garlic cloves
1 tablespoon vegetable oil
5 spring onions (scallions), sliced
125 ml (4 fl oz/½ cup) coconut cream
500 ml (17 fl oz/2 cups) chicken stock
2 lemon grass stems, white part only, bruised
875 ml (30 fl oz/3½ cups) coconut milk
750 g (1 lb 10 oz) pumpkin (winter squash), cut into 2 cm (¾ inch) cubes
1 tablespoon fish sauce
4 tablespoons Thai basil leaves

SERVES 4

Peel the prawns and gently pull out the dark vein from each prawn back, starting from the head end.

Wrap the shrimp paste in foil and put under a hot grill (broiler) for 1 minute. Unwrap the foil and put the shrimp paste in a food processor with the chilli, peppercorns, chilli paste, garlic and a pinch of salt, and process until smooth. Set aside.

Heat a wok over high heat, add the oil and swirl to coat the side. Cook the spring onion for 1–2 minutes, or until lightly golden, then remove from the wok. Set aside. Add the coconut cream and bring to the boil over high heat, then simmer for 10 minutes, or until the oil starts to separate from the cream — this is called cracking.

Stir in the processed paste and simmer over medium heat for 1–2 minutes, or until fragrant. Add the stock, lemon grass, coconut milk, pumpkin and cooked spring onion, cover with a lid and simmer for 8–10 minutes, or until the pumpkin is tender. Remove the lid, add the prawns and cook for a further 2–3 minutes, or until cooked through. Stir in the fish sauce and basil and serve.

PREPARATION TIME: 20 MINUTES   COOKING TIME: 30 MINUTES

GARLIC SOUP

1 garlic bulb
2 large thyme sprigs
1 litre (35 fl oz/4 cups) chicken stock
80 ml (2½ fl oz/⅓ cup) pouring (whipping) cream
4 thick slices white bread, crusts removed
thyme, extra, to garnish

SERVES 4

Preheat the oven to 180°C (350°F/Gas 4). Crush the cloves (about 20) from the garlic bulb, using the side of a knife. Discard the skin and put the garlic in a large saucepan with the thyme sprigs, chicken stock and 250 ml (9 fl oz/1 cup) water. Bring to the boil, then reduce the heat and simmer, uncovered, for 20 minutes. Strain through a fine sieve into a clean saucepan. Add the cream and reheat gently without allowing to boil. Season to taste.

Meanwhile, cut the bread into bite-sized cubes. Spread on a baking tray and bake for 5–10 minutes, or until lightly golden. Distribute among four soup bowls, then pour the soup over the bread. Garnish with extra thyme and serve immediately.

PREPARATION TIME: 15 MINUTES   COOKING TIME: 45 MINUTES

Thai pumpkin and coconut soup

CORN AND CRAB SOUP WITH CORIANDER

1½ tablespoons oil
6 garlic cloves, chopped
6 red Asian shallots, chopped
2 lemon grass stems, white part only, chopped
1 tablespoon grated fresh ginger
1 litre (35 fl oz/4 cups) chicken stock
250 ml (9 fl oz/1 cup) coconut milk
375 g (13 oz/2½ cups) corn kernels
350 g (12 oz) tinned crabmeat, drained
2 tablespoons fish sauce
2 tablespoons lime juice
1 teaspoon grated palm sugar (jaggery) or brown sugar
coriander (ciantro) leaves, to garnish
sliced chilli (optional), to serve

SERVES 4

Heat the oil in a large saucepan. Add the garlic, Asian shallots, lemon grass and grated ginger to the pan and stir over medium heat for 2 minutes. Add the stock and coconut milk to the pan and bring to the boil. Add the corn and cook for 5 minutes. Add the crabmeat, fish sauce, lime juice and sugar and stir.

Season to taste and serve immediately, topped with coriander leaves, and sliced chillies, if desired.

PREPARATION TIME: 15 MINUTES   COOKING TIME: 10 MINUTES

PUMPKIN SOUP WITH HARISSA

2.5 kg (5 lb 8 oz) pumpkin (winter squash)
750 ml (26 fl oz/3 cups) vegetable stock
750 ml (26 fl oz/3 cups) milk
sugar, to taste

HARISSA
250 g (9 oz) fresh or dried red chillies
1 tablespoon caraway seeds
1 tablespoon coriander seeds
2 teaspoons cumin seeds
4-6 garlic cloves
1 tablespoon dried mint
125 ml (4 fl oz/½ cup) extra virgin olive oil

SERVES 6

Remove the skin, seeds and fibre from the pumpkin and cut into pieces. Simmer, uncovered, in a large saucepan with the stock and milk for 15-20 minutes or until tender. Allow to cool slightly before transferring to a food processor, and blending, in batches, until smooth. Season with a little sugar and black pepper. Return to a clean saucepan and gently reheat until ready to serve.

To make the harissa, wearing rubber gloves, remove the stems of the chillies, split in half, remove the seeds and soften the flesh in hot water for 5 minutes (or 30 minutes if using dried). Drain and place in a food processor.

While the chillies are soaking, dry-fry the caraway, coriander and cumin seeds in a frying pan for 1-2 minutes, or until they become aromatic. Add the seeds, garlic, mint and 1 teaspoon salt to the food processor and, slowly adding the olive oil, process until a smooth, thick paste forms. Stir the harissa into individual bowls of soup to suit tastes.

PREPARATION TIME: 10-40 MINUTES   COOKING TIME: 20 MINUTES

PRAWN BISQUE

500 g (1 lb 2 oz) raw prawns (shrimp)
60 g (2¼ oz) butter
2 tablespoons plain (all-purpose) flour
2 litres (70 fl oz/8 cups) fish stock
½ teaspoon paprika
250 ml (9 fl oz/1 cup) pouring (whipping) cream
80 ml (2½ fl oz/⅓ cup) dry sherry
1-2 tablespoons pouring (whipping) cream, extra, to serve
paprika, extra, to garnish

SERVES 4-6

Peel the prawns and gently pull out the dark vein from each prawn back, starting at the head end. Reserve the heads and shells.

Heat the butter in a saucepan, add the prawn heads and shells and cook, stirring, over medium heat for 5 minutes, lightly crushing the heads with a wooden spoon. Add the flour and stir until combined. Add the fish stock and paprika and stir over the heat until the mixture boils. Reduce the heat and simmer, covered, over low heat, for 10 minutes. Strain the mixture through a fine sieve, then return the liquid to the pan. Add the prawns and cook over low heat for 2-3 minutes. Allow to cool slightly, then transfer to a food processor and blend, in batches, until smooth. Return the mixture to the pan. Add the cream and sherry to the pan and stir to heat through. Season to taste. Serve topped with a swirl of cream and sprinkled with paprika.

PREPARATION TIME: 25 MINUTES   COOKING TIME: 15-20 MINUTES

Pumpkin soup with harissa

LOBSTER BISQUE

1 raw lobster tail, about 400 g (14 oz)
90 g (3¼ oz) butter
1 large onion, chopped
1 large carrot, chopped
1 celery stalk, chopped
60 ml (2 fl oz/¼ cup) brandy
250 ml (9 fl oz/1 cup) white wine
6 parsley sprigs
1 thyme sprig
2 bay leaves
1 tablespoon tomato paste (concentrated purée)
1 litre (35 fl oz/4 cups) fish stock
2 tomatoes, chopped
2 tablespoons rice flour or cornflour (cornstarch)
125 ml (4 fl oz/½ cup) pouring (whipping) cream

SERVES 4–6

Remove the meat from the lobster tail. Wash the shell and crush into large pieces with a mallet or rolling pin, then set aside. Chop the meat into small pieces, cover and chill.

Melt the butter in a large saucepan, add the onion, carrot and celery and cook over low heat for 20 minutes, stirring occasionally, until the vegetables are softened but not brown.

In a small saucepan, heat the brandy, set alight with a long match and carefully pour over the vegetables. Shake the pan until the flame dies down. Add the white wine and the lightly crushed lobster shell. Increase the heat and boil until the liquid is reduced by half. Add the parsley, thyme, bay leaves, tomato paste, fish stock and chopped tomato. Simmer, uncovered, for 25 minutes, stirring occasionally. Strain the mixture through a fine sieve or dampened muslin (cheesecloth), pressing gently to extract all the liquid. Discard the vegetables and lobster shell. Return the liquid to a cleaned pan.

Blend the rice flour or cornflour with the cream in a small bowl. Add to the liquid and stir over medium heat until the mixture boils and thickens. Add the lobster meat and season to taste. Cook, without boiling, for 10 minutes, or until the lobster is just cooked. Serve hot.

PREPARATION TIME: 20 MINUTES   COOKING TIME: 1 HOUR

NOTE: If you don't dampen the muslin when straining the mixture, it will soak up too much of the liquid.

FRAGRANT CORN, COCONUT AND CHICKEN NOODLE SOUP

100 g (3½ oz) dried rice vermicelli
250 ml (9 fl oz/1 cup) coconut cream
500 ml (17 fl oz/2 cups) coconut milk
250 ml (9 fl oz/1 cup) chicken stock
125 g (4½ oz) tinned creamed corn
500 g (1 lb 2 oz) chicken thigh fillets,
cut into 2 cm (¾ inch) cubes
200 g (7 oz) baby corn, halved lengthways
5 cm (2 inch) piece of galangal, sliced
6 makrut (kaffir lime) leaves, shredded
2 lemon grass stems, white part only,
bruised and cut into 5 cm (2 inch) pieces
2 tablespoons fish sauce
2 tablespoons lime juice
1 tablespoon grated palm sugar (jaggery)
or soft brown sugar
15 g (½ oz) coriander (cilantro) leaves

SERVES 4

Soak the vermicelli in boiling water for 6–7 minutes, or until soft. Drain and set aside.

Put the coconut cream, coconut milk, chicken stock and creamed corn in a large saucepan and bring to the boil, then reduce the heat and simmer for 5 minutes. Add the chicken, baby corn, galangal, lime leaves and lemon grass and simmer for 10 minutes, or until the chicken is cooked.

Season with fish sauce, lime juice and palm sugar. Stir through half the coriander leaves and serve topped with the remaining leaves.

PREPARATION TIME: 20 MINUTES +   COOKING TIME: 20 MINUTES

CORN CHOWDER

90 g (3¼ oz) butter
2 large onions, finely chopped
1 garlic clove, crushed
2 teaspoons cumin seeds
1 litre (35 fl oz/4 cups) vegetable stock
2 potatoes, chopped
250 g (9 oz/1 cup) tinned creamed corn
400 g (14 oz/2 cups) corn kernels
3 tablespoons chopped flat-leaf (Italian)
parsley
125 g (4½ oz/1 cup) grated cheddar cheese
2 tablespoons snipped chives, to garnish

SERVES 8

Heat the butter in large heavy-based saucepan. Add the onions and cook over medium-high heat for 5 minutes, or until golden. Add the garlic and cumin seeds, cook for 1 minute, stirring constantly. Add the vegetable stock and bring to the boil. Add the potatoes and reduce the heat. Simmer, uncovered, for 10 minutes.

Add the creamed corn, corn kernels and parsley. Bring to the boil, then reduce the heat and simmer for 10 minutes. Stir through the cheese and season to taste. Heat gently until the cheese melts.

Serve immediately, sprinkled with the chives.

PREPARATION TIME: 15 MINUTES   COOKING TIME: 30 MINUTES

Fragrant corn, coconut and chicken noodle soup

CHICKEN LAKSA

1½ tablespoons coriander seeds

1 tablespoon cumin seeds

1 teaspoon ground turmeric

1 onion, roughly chopped

1 tablespoon roughly chopped ginger

3 garlic cloves

3 lemon grass stems, white part only, sliced

6 macadamia nuts

4–6 small red chillies

3 teaspoons shrimp paste, roasted (see Note)

1 litre (35 fl oz/4 cups) chicken stock

60 ml (2 fl oz/¼ cup) oil

400 g (14 oz) chicken thigh fillets, cut into 2 cm (¾ inch) pieces

750 ml (26 fl oz/3 cups) coconut milk

4 makrut (kaffir lime) leaves

2½ tablespoons lime juice

2 tablespoons fish sauce

2 tablespoons grated palm sugar (jaggery) or soft brown sugar

250 g (9 oz) dried rice vermicelli

90 g (3¼ oz/1 cup) bean sprouts, trimmed

4 fried tofu puffs, cut into thin batons

3 tablespoons chopped Vietnamese mint

1 handful coriander (cilantro) leaves

lime wedges, to serve

SERVES 4–6

Toast the coriander and cumin seeds in a frying pan over medium heat for 1–2 minutes, or until fragrant, tossing the pan constantly to prevent them from burning. Grind finely using a mortar and pestle or a spice grinder.

Put all the spices, onion, ginger, garlic, lemon grass, macadamia nuts, chillies and shrimp paste in a food processor or blender. Add 125 ml (4 fl oz/½ cup) of the stock and blend to a paste.

Heat the oil in a wok or large saucepan over low heat and gently cook the paste for 3–5 minutes, stirring constantly to prevent it burning or sticking to the bottom of the pan. Add the remaining stock and bring to the boil over high heat. Reduce the heat to medium and simmer for 15 minutes, or until reduced slightly. Add the chicken and simmer for 4–5 minutes. Add the coconut milk, lime leaves, lime juice, fish sauce and palm sugar and simmer for 5 minutes over medium–low heat. Do not bring to the boil or cover with a lid, as the coconut milk will split.

Meanwhile, put the vermicelli in a heatproof bowl, cover with boiling water and soak for 6–7 minutes, or until softened. Drain and divide among large serving bowls with the bean sprouts. Ladle the hot soup over the top and garnish with some tofu strips, mint and coriander leaves. Serve with a wedge of lime.

PREPARATION TIME: 30 MINUTES +   COOKING TIME: 35 MINUTES

NOTE: To roast the shrimp paste, wrap the paste in foil and put under a hot grill (broiler) for 1 minute.

RISSONI AND MUSHROOM BROTH

90 g (3¼ oz) butter
2 garlic cloves, sliced
2 large onions, sliced
375 g (13 oz) mushrooms, thinly sliced
1.25 litres (44 fl oz/5 cups) chicken stock
125 g (4½ oz) rissoni
310 ml (10¾ fl oz/1¼ cups) pouring (whipping) cream

SERVES 4

Melt the butter in a large saucepan over low heat. Add the garlic and onion and cook for 1 minute. Add the sliced mushrooms and cook gently, without colouring, for 5 minutes. (Set aside a few mushroom slices to use as a garnish.) Add the chicken stock and cook for 10 minutes. Allow to cool slightly before transferring to a food processor and blending until smooth.

Meanwhile, add the rissoni in a large saucepan of rapidly boiling salted water and cook until *al dente*. Drain and set aside.

Return the soup to a clean pan and stir in the rissoni and cream. Heat through and season to taste. Garnish with the reserved mushrooms.

PREPARATION TIME: 15 MINUTES   COOKING TIME: 20–25 MINUTES

PRAWN AND BASIL SOUP

500 g (1 lb 2 oz) raw prawns (shrimp)
2 tablespoons olive oil
20 g (¾ oz) butter
2 garlic cloves
1 small red onion, thinly sliced
2 celery stalks, cut into thin batons
3 small carrots, cut into thin batons
1 tablespoon finely chopped flat-leaf (Italian) parsley
1½ tablespoons finely chopped basil
pinch cayenne pepper
125 ml (4 fl oz/½ cup) dry sherry
1 litre (35 fl oz/4 cups) chicken stock
70 g (2½ oz) conchiglie (shell pasta)
60 ml (2 fl oz/¼ cup) pouring (whipping) cream

SERVES 4

Peel the prawns and gently pull out the dark vein from each prawn back, starting from the head end.

In a large saucepan, heat the oil and butter. Add the garlic cloves and the onion and cook over low heat for 2–3 minutes. Add the celery and carrot and fry until the vegetables are golden, but not brown. Add the parsley, basil and cayenne pepper. Stir briefly, add the prawns and toss through. Remove the garlic cloves. Pour in the sherry, increase the heat and cook for 2–3 minutes. Add the chicken stock, bring back to the boil, reduce the heat and simmer for 5 minutes. Add the conchiglie and simmer until the pasta is *al dente*. Stir in the cream and season to taste.

PREPARATION TIME: 45 MINUTES   COOKING TIME: 15–20 MINUTES

Rissoni and mushroom broth

SMOKED HADDOCK CHOWDER

500 g (1 lb 2 oz) smoked haddock or cod
1 potato, diced
1 celery stalk, chopped
1 onion, finely chopped
50 g (1³/₄ oz) butter
1 bacon slice, finely chopped
2 tablespoons plain (all-purpose) flour
½ teaspoon dried mustard
½ teaspoon worcestershire sauce
250 ml (9 fl oz/1 cup) milk
3 tablespoons chopped flat-leaf (Italian) parsley
60 ml (2 fl oz/¼ cup) pouring (whipping) cream (optional)

SERVES 4–6

To make the fish stock, put the fish in a deep frying pan, add 1.25 litres (44 fl oz/5 cups) water and bring to the boil. Reduce the heat and simmer for 8 minutes, or until the fish flakes easily. Drain and reserve the stock. Discard the skin and bones and flake the fish. Set aside.

Put the potato, celery and onion in a saucepan with 750 ml (26 fl oz/ 3 cups) reserved stock. Bring to the boil, reduce the heat and simmer for 8 minutes, or until the vegetables are tender. Set aside.

Melt the butter in a large saucepan over low heat, add the bacon and stir for 3 minutes. Stir in the flour, mustard and worcestershire sauce and cook for 1 minute, or until pale and foaming. Remove from the heat and gradually stir in the milk. Return to the heat and stir until the chowder boils and thickens. Reduce the heat and simmer for 2 minutes. Stir in the vegetables and stock mixture, then add the parsley and fish. Simmer over low heat for 5 minutes, or until heated through. Season to taste and serve with cream.

PREPARATION TIME: 20 MINUTES   COOKING TIME: 35 MINUTES

GREEN PEA SOUP

335 g (11¾ oz/1½ cups) dried green
split peas
2 tablespoons oil
1 onion, finely chopped
1 celery stalk, finely sliced
1 carrot, finely sliced
1 tablespoon ground cumin
1 tablespoon ground coriander
2 teaspoons grated fresh ginger
1.25 litres (44 fl oz/5 cups) vegetable stock
310 g (11 oz/2 cups) frozen green peas
1 tablespoon chopped mint
yoghurt or sour cream, to serve

SERVES 4–6

Soak the split peas in cold water for 2 hours. Drain the peas well.

Heat the oil in a large heavy-based saucepan and add the onion, celery and carrot. Cook over medium heat for 3 minutes, stirring occasionally, until soft but not browned. Stir in the cumin, coriander and ginger, then cook for 1 minute. Add the split peas and stock to pan. Bring to the boil, then reduce the heat to low. Simmer, covered, for 1½ hours, stirring occasionally. Add the frozen peas to the pan and stir to combine.

Allow to cool slightly before transferring to a food processor and blending, in batches, until smooth. Return to a clean pan and gently reheat. Season to taste and then stir in the mint. Serve in bowls with a swirl of yoghurt or sour cream.

PREPARATION TIME: 20 MINUTES +   COOKING TIME: 1 HOUR 40 MINUTES

FISH SOUP WITH NOODLES

750 g (1 lb 10 oz) skinless firm white fish
fillets, cut into 3 cm (1¼ inch) pieces
2 teaspoons ground turmeric
3 lemon grass stems
80 ml (2½ fl oz/⅓ cup) peanut oil
2 onions, finely sliced
6 garlic cloves, crushed
2 teaspoons finely chopped fresh ginger
2 teaspoons paprika
1 tablespoon rice flour
500 ml (17 fl oz/2 cups) coconut milk
125 ml (4 fl oz/½ cup) fish sauce
500 g (1 lb 2 oz) somen noodles

GARNISHES
4 hard-boiled eggs, quartered
chopped coriander (cilantro) leaves
finely sliced spring onion (scallion)
4 limes, quartered
fish sauce, to taste
4 tablespoons chilli flakes
80 g (2¾ oz/½ cup) unsalted roasted
peanuts, roughly chopped

SERVES 8

Place the fish pieces on a plate and sprinkle with 1½ teaspoons salt and the turmeric. Set aside for 10 minutes.

Trim the lemon grass stems to about 18 cm (7 inches) long. Bruise the white fleshy ends so that the fragrance will be released during cooking, and tie the stems into loops.

Heat the peanut oil in a large saucepan. Add the onion and cook over medium heat for 10 minutes, or until soft and lightly golden. Add the garlic and ginger and cook for 1 minute. Add the fish, paprika and rice flour and combine well. Pour in 1.5 litres (52 fl oz/6 cups) water, the coconut milk and fish sauce, and stir. Add the loops of lemon grass and simmer for 10 minutes, or until the fish is cooked.

Meanwhile, cook the noodles in a large saucepan of boiling water for 8–10 minutes, or until tender. Drain.

Place a mound of noodles in eight warm individual serving bowls and ladle over the fish soup. Offer the garnishes in separate small bowls so the diners can add them to their own taste.

PREPARATION TIME: 40 MINUTES   COOKING TIME: 25 MINUTES

CREAMY CORN AND TOMATO SOUP

1 teaspoon olive oil
1 teaspoon vegetable stock (bouillon) powder
1 onion, finely chopped
3 tomatoes
425 g (15 oz) tomato paste (concentrated purée)
310 g (11 oz) tinned creamed corn
125 g (4½ oz) tinned corn kernels, drained
chilli powder, to taste
sour cream and tortillas, to serve

Heat the oil in a large saucepan. Add the stock powder and onion and cook until the onion is soft.

Score a cross in the base of the tomatoes. Put in a heatproof bowl and cover with boiling water. Leave for 30 seconds, then transfer to cold water and peel the skin away from the cross. Cut the tomato in half, scoop out the seeds and chop the flesh.

Add the tomato to the pan with the tomato paste, creamed corn and corn kernels. Season with chilli. Stir until heated through. Serve with a dollop of sour cream and some warm tortillas.

SERVES 4–6   PREPARATION TIME: 20 MINUTES   COOKING TIME: 15 MINUTES

TURKEY AND CORN SOUP

20 g (¾ oz) butter
1 leek, white part only, thinly sliced
875 ml (30 fl oz/3½ cups) chicken stock
425 g (15 oz) tinned creamed corn
250 g (9 oz) shredded cooked turkey

Melt the butter in a large saucepan, add the leek and stir over medium heat for 5 minutes, or until soft. Add the chicken stock and creamed corn and stir through. Season to taste. Bring to the boil, then reduce the heat and simmer, covered, for 5 minutes. Add the turkey to the pan and stir until heated through. Serve immediately.

SERVES 4   PREPARATION TIME: 10 MINUTES   COOKING TIME: 20 MINUTES

Creamy corn and tomato soup

NEW ENGLAND CLAM CHOWDER

1.5 kg (3 lb 5 oz) clams (vongole) or pipis,
in shell
2 teaspoons oil
3 bacon slices, chopped
1 onion, chopped
1 garlic clove, crushed
750 g (1 lb 10 oz) potatoes, cut into dice
310 ml (10³/4 fl oz/1¹/4 cups) fish stock
500 ml (17 fl oz/2 cups) milk
125 ml (4 fl oz/¹/2 cup) pouring (whipping)
cream
3 tablespoons chopped flat-leaf (Italian)
parsley

SERVES 4

Discard any clams that are broken, already open or do not close when tapped on the bench. If necessary, soak in cold water for 1–2 hours to remove any grit. Drain and put in a large heavy-based saucepan with 250 ml (9 fl oz/1 cup) water. Cover and simmer over low heat for 5 minutes, or until open. Discard any that do not open. Strain and reserve the liquid. Remove the clam meat from the shells.

Heat the oil in a clean saucepan. Add the bacon, onion and garlic and cook, stirring, over medium heat until the onion is soft and the bacon golden. Add the potato and stir well.

Measure the reserved clam liquid and add water to make 310 ml (10³/4 fl oz/1¹/4 cups). Add to the pan with the stock and milk. Bring to the boil, reduce the heat, cover and simmer 20 minutes, or until the potato is tender. Uncover and simmer for 10 minutes, or until slightly thickened. Add the cream, clam meat and parsley and season to taste. Heat through gently before serving, but do not allow to boil or the liquid may curdle.

PREPARATION TIME: 35 MINUTES +   COOKING TIME: 45 MINUTES

SPICY TOMATO AND PEA SOUP

5 large very ripe tomatoes, chopped
2 tablespoons ghee or butter
1 large onion, thinly sliced
1 garlic clove, crushed
2 teaspoons ground coriander
2 teaspoons ground cumin
1/2 teaspoon fennel seeds
2 bay leaves
1 green chilli, seeded and sliced
375 ml (13 fl oz/1½ cups) coconut cream
235 g (8½ oz/1½ cups) frozen peas
1 tablespoon sugar
1 tablespoon chopped mint

SERVES 6

In a saucepan, simmer the tomato in 500 ml (17 fl oz/2 cups) water until very tender. Allow to cool slightly before transferring to a food processor and blending, in batches, until smooth.

Heat the ghee in a large saucepan, add the onion and garlic and cook over medium heat until very soft. Add the coriander, cumin, fennel seeds, bay leaves and chilli, and cook, stirring, for 1 minute. Add the coconut cream and the pureed tomatoes, and bring to the boil. Reduce the heat, add the peas and cook until tender. Remove the bay leaves, add the sugar and mint, and season with freshly ground pepper to taste.

PREPARATION TIME: 15 MINUTES   COOKING TIME: 20–25 MINUTES

FISH AND NOODLE SOUP

200 g (7 oz) dried rice vermicelli
1 tablespoon oil
2.5 cm (1 inch) piece of ginger, grated
3 small red chillies, finely chopped
4 spring onions (scallions), chopped
875 ml (30 fl oz/3½ cups) coconut milk
2 tablespoons fish sauce
2 tablespoons tomato paste (concentrated purée)
500 g (1 lb 2 oz) skinless firm white fish fillets, cubed
2 ham steaks, diced
150 g (5½ oz) snake (yard-long) beans, chopped
185 g (6½ oz) bean sprouts, trimmed
1 small handful mint
80 g (2¾ oz/½ cup) unsalted roasted peanuts

SERVES 4

Soak the vermicelli in boiling water for 6–7 minutes, or until soft, then drain well.

Heat the oil in a large, heavy-based saucepan and cook the ginger, chilli and spring onion for 3 minutes, or until golden. Stir in the coconut milk, fish sauce and tomato paste, cover and simmer for 10 minutes. Add the fish, ham and snake beans and simmer for 10 minutes, or until the fish is tender.

Divide the vermicelli among four bowls and top with the bean sprouts and mint. Spoon the soup into the bowls and sprinkle with peanuts.

PREPARATION TIME: 15 MINUTES   COOKING TIME: 20 MINUTES

Spicy tomato and pea soup

COCONUT PRAWN SOUP

CURRY PASTE
6 long dried red chillies
2 teaspoons coriander seeds
1 teaspoon cumin seeds
1 teaspoon ground turmeric
½ teaspoon paprika
½ teaspoon black peppercorns
4 red Asian shallots, chopped
4 garlic cloves, roughly chopped
1 tablespoon sliced fresh ginger
4 coriander (cilantro) roots, well rinsed
2 tablespoons chopped coriander (cilantro) stems
1 teaspoon grated lime zest
2 lemon grass stems, white part only, sliced (reserve the stems for the stock)
2 makrut (kaffir lime) leaves, thinly shredded
1 teaspoon shrimp paste
2 tablespoons vegetable oil

STOCK
700 g (1 lb 9 oz) raw prawns (shrimp)
4 red Asian shallots, chopped
1 garlic clove
6 black peppercorns

2 tablespoons vegetable oil
800 ml (28 fl oz) coconut milk
60 ml (2 fl oz/¼ cup) fish sauce
coriander (cilantro) leaves, to garnish
thinly sliced lime zest, to garnish

SERVES 4

To make the curry paste, soak the chillies in boiling water for 20 minutes, then drain. Toss the spices and peppercorns in a frying pan over medium heat for 1 minute, or until fragrant. Grind to a powder using a mortar and pestle, then transfer to a food processor and add the remaining paste ingredients and 1 teaspoon salt. Process until smooth, adding a little water, if necessary.

Peel the prawns, leaving the tails intact. Gently pull out the dark vein from each prawn back, starting from the head end. Cover with plastic wrap and refrigerate. Reserve the heads and shells.

To make the stock, dry-fry the prawn heads and shells in a wok over high heat for 5 minutes, or until orange. Add the remaining stock ingredients and 1.5 litres (52 fl oz/6 cups) water and bring to the boil. Reduce the heat, simmer for 15–20 minutes, then strain into a bowl.

Heat a clean, dry wok over medium heat, add the oil and swirl to coat the side. Add 3 tablespoons of the curry paste and stir constantly over medium heat for 1–2 minutes, or until fragrant. Stir in the stock and coconut milk and bring to the boil, then reduce the heat and simmer for 10 minutes. Add the prawns and cook, stirring, for 2 minutes, or until they are cooked. Stir in the fish sauce and garnish with coriander leaves and lime zest.

PREPARATION TIME: 20 MINUTES +   COOKING TIME: 45 MINUTES

NOTE: Freeze the leftover curry paste in an airtight container.

MEAL IN A BOWL

MINESTRONE WITH PESTO

125 g (4½ oz) dried borlotti (cranberry) beans
60 ml (2 fl oz/¼ cup) olive oil
1 large onion, finely chopped
2 garlic cloves, crushed
60 g (2¼ oz) pancetta, finely chopped
1 celery stalk, halved lengthways and cut into thin slices
1 carrot, halved lengthways and cut into thin slices
1 potato, diced
2 teaspoons tomato paste (concentrated purée)
400 g (14 oz) tinned crushed tomatoes
6 basil leaves, roughly torn
2 litres (70 fl oz/8 cups) chicken or vegetable stock
2 zucchini (courgettes), cut into thin slices
115 g (4 oz/¾ cup) fresh peas, shelled
60 g (2¼ oz) green beans, cut into short lengths
80 g (2¾ oz) silverbeet (Swiss chard) leaves, shredded
3 tablespoons chopped flat-leaf (Italian) parsley
70 g (2½ oz) ditalini or other small pasta

PESTO
30 g (1 oz) basil leaves
20 g (¾ oz) lightly toasted pine nuts (see Note)
2 garlic cloves
100 ml (3½ fl oz) olive oil
25 g (1 oz/¼ cup) freshly grated parmesan cheese

SERVES 6

Soak the borlotti beans in plenty of cold water overnight. Drain and rinse thoroughly under cold water.

Heat the oil in a large, deep saucepan, add the onion, garlic and pancetta and cook over low heat, stirring occasionally, for 8–10 minutes, or until softened. Add the celery, carrot and potato and cook for 5 minutes. Stir in the tomato paste, tomatoes, basil and drained borlotti beans. Season to taste with freshly ground black pepper. Add the stock and bring slowly to the boil. Cover and simmer, stirring occasionally, for 1½ hours. Add the zucchini, peas, green beans, silverbeet, parsley and the pasta. Simmer for 8–10 minutes, or until the vegetables and pasta are *al dente*. Check for seasoning and adjust if necessary.

To make the pesto, combine the basil, pine nuts and garlic with a pinch of salt in a food processor. Process until finely chopped. With the motor running, slowing add the olive oil. Transfer to a bowl and stir in the parmesan and some ground black pepper to taste. Serve with the soup.

PREPARATION TIME: 25 MINUTES +   COOKING TIME: 2 HOURS

NOTE: Toast the pine nuts in a frying pan over medium heat, stirring constantly, until they are golden brown and fragrant. Watch carefully as they will burn easily.

THAI RICE NOODLE SOUP WITH DUCK

1 whole Chinese roast duck (see Note)

4 coriander (cilantro) roots and stems, well rinsed

50 g (1¾ oz) galangal, sliced

4 spring onions (scallions), sliced

400 g (14 oz) Chinese broccoli (gai larn), cut into 5 cm (2 inch) lengths

2 garlic cloves, crushed

60 ml (2 fl oz/¼ cup) fish sauce

1 tablespoon hoisin sauce

2 teaspoons grated palm sugar (jaggery) or soft brown sugar

½ teaspoon ground white pepper

500 g (1 lb 2 oz) fresh rice noodles

crisp fried garlic, to garnish (optional)

coriander (cilantro) leaves, to garnish (optional)

SERVES 4–6

To make the stock, cut off the duck's head with a sharp knife and discard. Remove the skin and fat from the duck, leaving the neck intact. Carefully remove the flesh from the bones and set aside. Cut any visible fat from the carcass along with the parson's nose then discard. Break the carcass into large pieces and put in a large stockpot with 2 litres (70 fl oz/8 cups) water.

Bruise the coriander roots and stems with the back of a knife. Add to the pot with the galangal and bring to the boil. Skim off any scum from the surface. Boil over medium heat for 10 minutes. Strain the stock through a fine sieve then discard the carcass and return the stock to a large clean wok.

Slice the duck flesh into strips. Add to the stock with the spring onion, Chinese broccoli, garlic, fish sauce, hoisin sauce, palm sugar and white pepper. Gently bring to the boil.

Put the noodles in a heatproof bowl, cover with boiling water and gently separate. Drain well and refresh under cold water. Divide the noodles evenly among the serving bowls and pour over the soup. If desired, garnish with the fried garlic and coriander leaves. Serve immediately.

PREPARATION TIME: 40 MINUTES   COOKING TIME: 25 MINUTES

NOTE: Whole Chinese roast duck is available from Chinese barbecue shops.

BOUILLABAISSE WITH ROUILLE

500 g (1 lb 2 oz) ripe tomatoes
60 ml (2 fl oz/¼ cup) olive oil
1 large onion, chopped
2 leeks, sliced
4 garlic cloves, crushed
1–2 tablespoons tomato paste
(concentrated purée)
6 flat-leaf (Italian) parsley sprigs
2 bay leaves
2 thyme sprigs
1 fennel sprig
2 pinches saffron threads
2 kg (4 lb 8 oz) fish trimmings (such as
heads, bones, shellfish remains)
1 tablespoon Pernod or Ricard
4 potatoes, cut into 1.5 cm (⅝ inch) slices
1.5 kg (3 lb 5 oz) mixed fish fillets (such as
rascasse, snapper, blue eye and
bream), cut into large chunks
(see Note)
2 tablespoons chopped flat-leaf (Italian)
parsley

TOASTS
12 slices of baguette
2 large garlic cloves, sliced in half

ROUILLE
3 slices white bread, crusts removed
1 red capsicum (pepper), seeded,
membrane removed and quartered
1 small red chilli, seeded and chopped
3 garlic cloves, crushed
1 tablespoon shredded basil
80 ml (2½ fl oz/⅓ cup) olive oil

SERVES 6

Score a cross in the base of each tomato. Put in a heatproof bowl and cover with boiling water. Leave for 30 seconds then transfer to cold water, drain and peel away the skin from the cross and roughly chop the flesh.

Heat the oil in a large saucepan over medium heat, add the onion and leek and cook for 5 minutes without browning. Add the garlic, tomato and 1 tablespoon tomato paste, reduce the heat and simmer for 5 minutes. Stir in 2 litres (70 fl oz/8 cups) cold water then add the parsley, bay leaves, thyme, fennel, saffron and fish trimmings. Bring to the boil, then reduce the heat and simmer for 30 minutes. Strain the stock into a large saucepan, pressing the juices out of the ingredients and reserving 2 tablespoons of stock for the rouille.

Add the Pernod to the saucepan and stir in the extra tomato paste. Season, then bring to the boil and add the potato. Reduce the heat and simmer for 5 minutes. Add the firmer-fleshed fish to the saucepan and cook for 2–3 minutes, then add the more delicate pieces of fish and cook for a further 5 minutes.

Meanwhile, toast the bread until golden on both sides. While warm, rub the surfaces with the garlic.

To make the rouille, soak the bread in cold water for 5 minutes. Cook the capsicum pieces, skin side up, under a hot grill (broiler) until the skin blackens and blisters. Cool in a plastic bag, then peel. Roughly chop the flesh. Squeeze the bread dry and place in a food processor with the capsicum, chilli, garlic and basil. Process to a smooth paste. With the motor running, gradually add the oil until the consistency resembles mayonnaise. Thin with 1–2 tablespoons of the stock. Season to taste.

To serve, place two pieces of toast in each soup bowl. Spoon in the soup and fish. Sprinkle with parsley. Serve the rouille on the side.

PREPARATION TIME: 35 MINUTES   COOKING TIME: 1 HOUR 10 MINUTES

NOTE: Use at least four different fish with a range of textures and flavours. Shellfish such as lobster, crab, scallops or mussels can be used.

FISH BALL AND NOODLE SOUP

500 g (1 lb 2 oz) skinless, boneless firm white fish fillets, such as ling or perch

2 tablespoons rice flour

200 g (7 oz) dried somen noodles

2½ teaspoons dashi granules

2 tablespoons light soy sauce

1 tablespoon mirin

200 g (7 oz) Chinese cabbage (wong bok) shredded

2 spring onions (scallions), thinly sliced, to garnish

½ Lebanese (short) cucumber, peeled, seeded and cut into 5 cm (2 inch) strips, to garnish

SERVES 4–6

Put the fish in a food processor and process until smooth. Combine the rice flour and 80 ml (2½ fl oz/⅓ cup) water in a small bowl until smooth then add to the fish and process for 5 seconds. Using 2 teaspoons of mixture at a time, shape into balls with wet hands.

Cook the noodles in a large saucepan of boiling water for 2 minutes, or until tender. Drain and set aside.

Pour 2 litres (70 fl oz/8 cups) water into a non-stick wok and bring to the boil. Reduce the heat to low, add the dashi granules and stir until dissolved. Increase the heat to high and bring to the boil then add the soy sauce, mirin and salt to taste. Add the fish balls, reduce the heat to medium and simmer for 3 minutes, or until they rise to the surface and are cooked through. Add the Chinese cabbage, increase the heat to high and return to the boil. Stir in the noodles and cook for 1 minute, or until warmed through.

To serve, divide the noodles and fish balls among the serving bowls then ladle the liquid over the top. Sprinkle with the spring onion and cucumber.

PREPARATION TIME: 15 MINUTES   COOKING TIME: 15 MINUTES

CHINESE COMBINATION SHORT SOUP

STOCK
1.5 kg (3 lb 5 oz) whole chicken
60 ml (2 fl oz/¼ cup) Chinese rice wine
½ star anise
8 spring onions (scallions), chopped
2 leafy celery tops
½ teaspoon white peppercorns
4 garlic cloves, bruised
2 x 10 cm (¾ x 4 inch) piece fresh ginger,
thinly sliced

12 raw prawns (shrimp)
24 won tons
200 g (7 oz) Chinese barbecued pork,
thinly sliced
60 g (2¼ oz) Chinese straw mushrooms
70 g (2½ oz) sliced bamboo shoots
500 g (1 lb 2 oz) baby bok choy
(pak choy), thinly sliced
2 spring onions (scallions), cut into 3 cm
(1¼ inch) lengths
2½ tablespoons light soy sauce
1 tablespoon oyster sauce
½ teaspoon sesame oil

SERVES 4–6

Put all the stock ingredients in a stockpot and cover with 4 litres (140 fl oz/ 16 cups) water. Bring to the boil over high heat and skim off any scum that forms on the surface. Reduce the heat and simmer for 2 hours. Cool slightly then remove the chicken and strain the stock into a bowl. Cover and refrigerate the meat and stock separately until chilled. Skim off the fat from the top of the stock.

Meanwhile, remove one breast from the chicken then discard the skin and thinly slice the flesh. Peel the prawns and gently pull out the dark vein from each prawn back, starting from the head end.

Pour 2 litres (70 fl oz/4 cups) of the stock into a large wok and bring to the boil. Add the won tons and cook for 2–3 minutes, or until they have risen to the surface and are cooked. Remove with a slotted spoon and divide among serving bowls. Reduce the stock to a simmer, add the prawns, pork, mushrooms and bamboo shoots and cook for 30 seconds, or until the prawns are just curled. Add the bok choy, spring onion, chicken and the combined soy sauce, oyster sauce and sesame oil and cook for 2 minutes, or until the prawns are completely cooked. Ladle the soup over the won tons and serve.

PREPARATION TIME: 20 MINUTES +   COOKING TIME: 2 HOURS 20 MINUTES

RATATOUILLE AND PASTA SOUP

1 eggplant (aubergine)
2 tablespoons olive oil
1 large onion, chopped
1 large red capsicum (pepper), chopped
1 large green capsicum (pepper), chopped
2 garlic cloves, crushed
3 zucchini (courgettes), sliced
800 g (1 lb 12 oz) tinned crushed tomatoes
1 teaspoon dried oregano leaves
½ teaspoon dried thyme leaves
1 litre (35 fl oz/4 cups) vegetable stock
50 g (1¾ oz) fusilli
fresh parmesan cheese shavings, to serve

SERVES 6

Chop the eggplant. To remove any bitterness, spread the eggplant pieces out in a colander and sprinkle generously with salt. Set aside for 20 minutes and then rinse thoroughly and pat dry with paper towels.

Heat the oil in a large heavy-based saucepan and cook the onion over medium heat for 10 minutes, or until soft and lightly golden. Add the peppers, garlic, zucchini and eggplant and stir-fry for 5 minutes. Add the tomatoes, herbs and vegetable stock. Bring to the boil, reduce the heat and simmer for 10 minutes, or until the vegetables are tender. Add the fusilli and cook for a further 15 minutes, or until the fusilli is tender. Serve with shavings of parmesan scattered on top.

PREPARATION TIME: 25 MINUTES +   COOKING TIME: 40 MINUTES

PASTA AND BEAN SOUP

250 g (9 oz) borlotti (cranberry) beans, soaked in water overnight
1 ham hock
1 onion, chopped
pinch ground cinnamon
pinch cayenne pepper
2 teaspoons olive oil
500 ml (17 fl oz/2 cups) chicken stock
125 g (4½ oz) tagliatelle (plain or spinach), broken into short lengths

SERVES 4–6

Drain and rinse the borlotti beans, cover with cold water in a saucepan and bring to the boil. Stir, lower the heat and simmer for 15 minutes.

Drain the beans and transfer to a large saucepan with a tight-fitting lid. Add the ham hock, onion, cinnamon, cayenne, olive oil and stock, and enough cold water to cover. Cover and simmer over low heat for 1 hour, or until the beans are cooked and have begun to thicken the stock. Remove the hock and cut off any meat. Chop the meat and return it to the pan, discarding the bone. Season to taste.

When ready to serve, bring the soup back to the boil, toss in the tagliatelle and cook until *al dente*. Remove the pan from the heat and set aside for 1–2 minutes before serving.

PREPARATION TIME: 20 MINUTES +   COOKING TIME: 1 HOUR 25 MINUTES

Ratatouille and pasta soup

BEEF PHO

2 litres (70 fl oz/8 cups) beef stock
1 star anise
4 cm (1½ inch) piece fresh ginger, sliced
2 pigs' trotters (cut in half)
½ onion, studded with 2 whole cloves
2 lemon grass stems, bruised
2 garlic cloves, crushed
¼ teaspoon ground white pepper
1 tablespoon fish sauce, plus extra, to serve
200 g (7 oz) fresh thin rice noodles
300 g (10½ oz) beef fillet, partially frozen, thinly sliced
90 g (3¼ oz/1 cup) bean sprouts, trimmed
2 spring onions (scallions), thinly sliced,
25 g (1 oz) chopped coriander (cilantro) leaves, plus extra, to serve
4 tablespoons chopped Vietnamese mint, plus extra, to serve
1 red chilli, thinly sliced, plus extra, to serve
2 limes, quartered

SERVES 4

Put the beef stock, star anise, ginger, pigs' trotters, onion, lemon grass, garlic and white pepper in a wok and bring to the boil. Reduce the heat to very low and simmer, covered, for 30 minutes. Strain, return to the wok and stir in the fish sauce.

Meanwhile, put the noodles in a heatproof bowl, cover with boiling water and gently separate. Drain well then refresh under cold running water. Divide the noodles among four deep soup bowls then top with beef strips, bean sprouts, spring onion, coriander, mint and chilli. Ladle over the broth.

Place the extra chilli, mint and coriander, the lime quarters and fish sauce in small bowls on a platter, serve with the soup and allow your guests to help themselves.

PREPARATION TIME: 15 MINUTES +   COOKING TIME: 35 MINUTES

SICHUAN BEEF NOODLE SOUP

1.5 litres (52 fl oz/6 cups) beef stock
1 tablespoon peanut oil
400 g (14 oz) chuck steak
½ cinnamon stick
2 star anise
1½ teaspoons sichuan peppercorns, crushed
1 tablespoon finely sliced fresh ginger
2 tablespoons dark soy sauce
1 tablespoon Chinese rice wine
1 tablespoon brown bean sauce
3 x 5 cm (1¼ x 2 inch) piece dried mandarin peel (see Note)
125 g (4½ oz) fresh thin egg noodles
3 spring onions (scallions), thinly sliced

SERVES 4

Pour the beef stock and 2 litres (70 fl oz/8 cups) water into a stockpot and simmer over low heat; keep warm until needed.

Heat a wok over high heat, add the oil and swirl to coat the base and side. Add the steak and sear it for 2–3 minutes on each side. Add the cinnamon stick, star anise, peppercorns, ginger, soy sauce, rice wine, bean sauce and mandarin peel. Pour in the hot broth then cover and bring to simmering point over medium heat. Reduce the heat to low and simmer, covered, for 2–2½ hours, or until the steak is tender (you should be able to shred it; if not, return to the simmer until tender).

Remove the steak and discard the mandarin peel. Meanwhile, cook the noodles in a large saucepan of boiling water for 1 minute to separate them. Drain. Just before serving, add the noodles to the broth and let them stand for 1–2 minutes, or until heated through. Shred the steak into bite-sized pieces and divide evenly among four large serving bowls. Ladle on the broth and noodles, sprinkle with spring onion and serve.

PREPARATION TIME: 10 MINUTES   COOKING TIME: 3 HOURS

NOTE: Dried citrus peel is one of the most important Chinese flavourings and the dried peel of mandarins, tangerines and oranges is sold at many Asian food stores.

PRAWN LAKSA

750 g (1 lb 10 oz) raw prawns (shrimp)

1½ tablespoons coriander seeds

1 tablespoon cumin seeds

1 teaspoon ground turmeric

1 onion, roughly chopped

2 teaspoons roughly chopped fresh ginger

3 garlic cloves

3 lemon grass stems, white part only, sliced

6 candlenuts or macadamia nuts, roughly chopped

4-6 small red chillies, roughly chopped

2-3 teaspoons shrimp paste

1 litre (35 fl oz/4 cups) chicken stock

60 ml (2 fl oz/¼ cup) vegetable oil

750 ml (26 fl oz/3 cups) coconut milk

4 fresh makrut (kaffir lime) leaves

2½ tablespoons lime juice

2 tablespoons fish sauce

2 tablespoons grated palm sugar (jaggery) or soft brown sugar

250 g (8 oz) dried rice vermicelli

90 g (3¼ oz/1 cup) bean sprouts, trimmed

4 fried tofu puffs, cut into thin strips

3 tablespoons chopped Vietnamese mint

1 small handful coriander (cilantro) leaves

lime wedges, to serve

SERVES 4–6

Peel the prawns, leaving the tails intact. Gently pull out the dark vein from each prawn back, starting from the head end.

Dry-fry the coriander seeds in a small frying pan over medium heat for 1–2 minutes, or until fragrant, tossing constantly. Grind finely using a mortar and pestle or spice grinder. Repeat the process with the cumin seeds.

Put the ground coriander and cumin, turmeric, onion, ginger, garlic, lemon grass, candlenuts, chilli and shrimp paste in a food processor or blender. Add about 125 ml (4 fl oz/½ cup) of the stock and blend to a fine paste.

Heat a wok over low heat, add the oil and swirl to coat the base and side. Cook the paste for 3–5 minutes, stirring constantly. Pour in the remaining stock and bring to the boil, then reduce the heat and simmer for 15 minutes, or until reduced slightly. Add the coconut milk, makrut leaves, lime juice, fish sauce and sugar and simmer for 5 minutes. Add the prawns and simmer for 2 minutes, or until pink and cooked. Do not boil or cover.

Meanwhile, soak the vermicelli in boiling water for 6–7 minutes, or until soft. Drain and divide among serving bowls along with most of the sprouts. Ladle on the hot soup then top with the tofu, mint, coriander and the remaining sprouts. Serve with lime wedges.

PREPARATION TIME: 30 MINUTES   COOKING TIME: 35 MINUTES

SALMON NABE

12 dried shiitake mushrooms

250 g (9 oz) firm tofu

½ Chinese cabbage (wong bok)

4 salmon cutlets

2 x 5 cm (2 inch) pieces tinned bamboo shoots

2 litres (70 fl oz/8 cups) dashi

80 ml (2½ fl oz/⅓ cup) shoyu (Japanese soy sauce)

60 ml (2 fl oz/¼ cup) mirin or sake

SESAME SEED SAUCE

100 g (3½ oz) white sesame seeds

2 teaspoons oil

125 ml (4 fl oz/½ cup) shoyu (Japanese soy sauce)

2 tablespoons mirin

3 teaspoons caster (superfine) sugar

½ teaspoon instant dashi granules

SERVES 3–4

Soak the mushrooms in warm water for 15 minutes, then drain. Cut the tofu into 12 squares. Coarsely shred the cabbage into 5 cm (2 inch) wide pieces.

Place the mushrooms, tofu, cabbage, salmon, bamboo shoots, dashi, shoyu, mirin and a pinch of salt in a large saucepan and bring to the boil. Reduce the heat, cover and simmer over medium heat for 15 minutes. Turn the salmon cutlets over and simmer for a further 15 minutes, or until tender.

To make the sesame seed sauce, toast the sesame seeds in a frying pan over medium heat for 3–4 minutes, shaking the pan gently, until the seeds are golden brown. Remove from the pan at once to prevent burning. Grind the seeds using a mortar and pestle until a paste is formed. Add the oil, if necessary, to assist in forming a paste. Mix the paste with the shoyu, mirin, sugar, dashi granules and 125 ml (4 fl oz/½ cup) warm water.

Pour the salmon nabe into warmed serving bowls and serve with the sesame seed sauce.

PREPARATION TIME: 20 MINUTES   COOKING TIME: 40 MINUTES

NOTE: This dish is traditionally cooked in a clay pot over a burner and served in the same pot. Diners dip the fish and vegetable pieces into the accompanying sauce and the broth is served in small bowls at the end of the meal.

EIGHT TREASURE SOUP

12 raw small prawns (shrimp)
4 dried shiitake mushrooms
125 ml (4 fl oz/½ cup) boiling water
1 tablespoon vegetable oil
1 teaspoon sesame oil
2 teaspoons finely chopped fresh ginger
1 tablespoon finely chopped spring onion (scallion)
60 g (2¼ oz) Chinese bacon or ham, cut into thin strips (see Note)
1 litre (35 fl oz/4 cups) chicken stock
1 tablespoon soy sauce
1 tablespoon rice wine
250 g (9 oz) boneless, skinless chicken breast
1 carrot, cut into 1 cm (½ inch) slices
200 g (7 oz) firm tofu, cut into 2 cm (¾ inch) cubes
50 g (1¾ oz) sliced tinned bamboo shoots
100 g (3½ oz) baby English spinach, chopped
2 spring onions, thinly sliced, to serve

SERVES 4–6

Peel the prawns. Gently pull out the dark vein from each prawn back, starting from the head end.

Soak the mushrooms in the boiling water for 20 minutes. Squeeze dry, reserving the soaking liquid. Discard the woody stalks and cut the caps into quarters.

Heat a wok over high heat. Add the oils and swirl to coat the base and side, then add the ginger, spring onion and bacon. Cook for 10 seconds before adding the stock, soy sauce, rice wine, mushroom liquid and ½ teaspoon salt. Bring to the boil and add the chicken. Reduce the heat to low, cover with a lid and poach the chicken for 20 minutes. Remove the chicken with a slotted spoon and, when cool enough to handle, shred the meat.

Return the stock to the boil, add the carrot and cook for 5 minutes. Add the prawns, tofu, bamboo shoots, spinach and chicken meat and cook over low heat for a further 5 minutes. Serve with the extra spring onion.

PREPARATION TIME: 15 MINUTES +   COOKING TIME: 1 HOUR

NOTE: Chinese bacon has a dryish flesh with a strong flavour very much like prosciutto. You can substitute prosciutto.

PORK AND BUTTERED CORN RAMEN NOODLE SOUP

200 g (7 oz) Chinese barbecued pork fillet, in one piece

2 small fresh corn cobs

200 g (7 oz) dried ramen noodles

2 teaspoons peanut oil

1 teaspoon grated fresh ginger

1.5 litres (52 fl oz/6 cups) chicken stock

2 tablespoons mirin

2 spring onions (scallions), sliced

20 g (³/4 oz) unsalted butter

1 spring onion (scallion), sliced, extra, to serve

SERVES 4

Cut the pork into thin slices. Cut the kernels from the corn cobs.

Cook the ramen noodles in a large saucepan of boiling water for 4 minutes, or until tender. Drain, rinse in cold water then drain again. Set aside.

Heat a wok over high heat, add the oil and swirl to coat the base and side. Stir-fry the ginger for 1 minute, then pour in the stock, mirin and 500 ml (17 fl oz/2 cups) water. Bring to the boil, then reduce the heat and simmer for 6-8 minutes. Add the pork to the broth and cook for 5 minutes. Add the corn kernels and spring onion and cook for a further 4-5 minutes, or until the kernels are tender.

Separate the noodles by running them under hot water then divide among four deep bowls, shaping them into mounds. Ladle over the liquid and top with the pork and corn. Place 1 teaspoon butter on top of each mound and garnish with the extra spring onion. Serve immediately.

PREPARATION TIME: 15 MINUTES   COOKING TIME: 30 MINUTES

SICHUAN SOUP

4 dried Chinese mushrooms

50 g (1³/4 oz) thick dried rice stick noodles

1 litre (35 fl oz/4 cups) chicken stock

175 g (6 oz/1 cup) cooked chicken, chopped

235 g (8¹/2 oz) tinned bamboo shoots, drained and chopped

1 teaspoon grated fresh ginger

1 tablespoon cornflour (cornstarch)

1 egg, lightly beaten

1 teaspoon tomato sauce (ketchup)

1 tablespoon soy sauce

1 tablespoon vinegar

2 teaspoons sesame oil

2 spring onions (scallions), finely chopped

SERVES 6-8

Cover the mushrooms with hot water and soak for 20 minutes. Drain thoroughly and chop. Soak the noodles in hot water for 20 minutes. Drain and cut into short lengths. Set aside.

Heat the stock in a large saucepan and bring to the boil. Add the mushrooms, noodles, chicken, bamboo shoots and ginger. Reduce the heat and simmer gently.

Combine the cornflour with 80 ml (2¹/2 oz/¹/3 cup) water in a small bowl and mix to a smooth paste. Add the cornflour mixture to the soup and stir until clear. Add the egg to the soup in a fine stream, stirring the mixture constantly. Remove the pan from the heat. Add the tomato sauce, soy sauce, vinegar, sesame oil and spring onion. Season to taste. Serve topped with extra spring onion, if desired.

PREPARATION TIME: 20 MINUTES +   COOKING TIME: 15 MINUTES

Pork and buttered corn ramen noodle soup

SOUPE AU PISTOU

2 ripe tomatoes
3 flat-leaf (Italian) parsley stalks
1 large rosemary sprig
1 large thyme sprig
1 large marjoram sprig
60 ml (2 fl oz/¼ cup) olive oil
2 onions, thinly sliced
1 leek, white part only, thinly sliced
1 bay leaf
375 g (13 oz) pumpkin (winter squash), cut into small pieces
250 g (9 oz) potato, cut into small pieces
1 carrot, halved lengthways and thinly sliced
2 litres (70 fl oz/8 cups) vegetable stock or water
90 g (3¼) oz) fresh or frozen broad (fava) beans
80 g (2¾ oz/½ cup) fresh or frozen peas
2 small zucchinis (courgettes), finely chopped
80 g (2¾ oz/½ cup) short macaroni or shell pasta

PISTOU
25 g (1 oz) basil leaves
2 large garlic cloves, crushed
80 ml (2½ fl oz/⅓ cup) olive oil
35 g (1¼ oz/⅓ cup) freshly grated parmesan cheese

SERVES 8

Score a cross in the base of each tomato. Put in a heatproof bowl and cover with boiling water. Leave for 30 seconds then transfer to cold water, drain, peel away the skin from the cross and chop the flesh. Tie the parsley, rosemary, thyme and marjoram together with string.

Heat the oil in a heavy-based saucepan and add the onion and leek. Cook over low heat for 10 minutes, or until soft. Add the herb bunch, bay leaf, pumpkin, potato, carrot, 1 teaspoon salt and the stock. Cover and simmer 10 minutes, or until vegetables are almost tender.

Add the broad beans, peas, zucchini, tomatoes and pasta. Cover and cook for 15 minutes, or until the vegetables are very tender and the pasta is *al dente*. Add more water if necessary. Remove the herbs, including the bay leaf.

To make the pistou, finely chop the basil and garlic in a food processor. Pour in the oil gradually, processing until smooth. Stir in the parmesan and ½ teaspoon freshly ground black pepper and serve spooned over the soup.

PREPARATION TIME: 45 MINUTES   COOKING TIME: 35 MINUTES

NOTE: The flavour of this soup improves if refrigerated overnight then gently reheated.

CANJA

3 tomatoes
2.5 litres (87 fl oz/10 cups) chicken stock
1 onion, cut into thin wedges
1 celery stalk, finely chopped
1 teaspoon grated lemon zest
1 mint sprig
1 tablespoon olive oil
2 boneless, skinless chicken breasts
200 g (7 oz/1 cup) long-grain rice
2 tablespoons lemon juice
2 tablespoons shredded mint

SERVES 6

Score a cross in the base of each tomato. Put in a heatproof bowl and cover with boiling water. Leave for 30 seconds then transfer to cold water, drain and peel away the skin from the cross. Cut the tomatoes in half, scoop out the seeds and roughly chop the flesh.

Combine the stock, onion, celery, lemon zest, tomato, mint and olive oil in a large saucepan. Slowly bring to the boil then reduce the heat, add the chicken and simmer gently for 20–25 minutes, or until the chicken is cooked through.

Remove the chicken from the saucepan and discard the mint sprig. Allow the chicken to cool, then thinly slice.

Meanwhile, add the rice to the pan and simmer for 25–30 minutes, or until the rice is tender. Return the sliced chicken to the pan, add the lemon juice and stir for 1–2 minutes, or until the chicken is warmed through. Season to taste and stir in the shredded mint just before serving.

PREPARATION TIME: 15 MINUTES   COOKING TIME: 1 HOUR

FAST SPICY BEAN SOUP

2 tablespoons oil
1 onion, chopped
2 garlic cloves, crushed
½ teaspoon chilli powder
850 g (1 lb 14 oz) tinned mixed beans, rinsed and drained
500 ml (17 fl oz/2 cups) vegetable stock
400 g (14 oz) tinned tomato passata (puréed tomatoes)
1 hard-boiled egg, finely chopped
finely chopped flat-leaf (Italian) parsley

SERVES 4

Heat the oil in a saucepan and fry the onion for 5 minutes, or until soft. Add the garlic and chilli powder, stir fry for 1 minute then add the mixed beans. Stir in the vegetable stock and tomato passata and cook until heated through. Season to taste. Garnish with the egg and parsley and serve.

PREPARATION TIME: 15 MINUTES   COOKING TIME: 20 MINUTES

NOTE: Combinations of beans such as red kidney, cannellini and haricot are available in tins. If you prefer, you can use just one kind of bean.

ZARZUELA

SOFRITO SAUCE
2 large tomatoes

1 tablespoon olive oil

2 onions, finely chopped

1 tablespoon tomato paste (concentrated purée)

PICADA SAUCE
3 slices white bread, crusts removed

1 tablespoon almonds, toasted

3 garlic cloves

1 tablespoon olive oil

1 raw lobster tail (about 400 g/14 oz)

12–15 black mussels

750 g (1 lb 10 oz) skinless firm white fish fillets, such as flake, cod or monkfish, cut into bite-sized pieces

plain (all-purpose) flour, seasoned

2–3 tablespoons olive oil

125 g (4¼ oz) calamari rings

12 large raw prawns (shrimp)

125 ml (4 fl oz/½ cup) white wine

125 ml (4 fl oz/½ cup) brandy

3 tablespoons chopped parsley, to garnish

SERVES 4

To make the sofrito sauce, score a cross in the base of each tomato. Put in a heatproof bowl and cover with boiling water. Leave for 30 seconds, then transfer to cold water and peel the skin away from the cross. Cut the tomatoes in half, scoop out the seeds and roughly chop the flesh.

Heat the oil in a saucepan over medium heat. Add the onion and stir for 5 minutes without browning. Add the tomato, tomato paste and 125 ml (4 fl oz/½ cup) water and stir over medium heat for 10 minutes. Stir in another 125 ml (4 fl oz/½ cup) water, season and set aside.

To make the picada sauce, finely chop the bread, almonds and garlic in a food processor. With the motor running, gradually add the oil to form a paste, adding another ½ tablespoon of oil if necessary.

Preheat the oven to 180°C (350°F/Gas 4). Cut the lobster tail into rounds through the membrane that separates the shell segments. Set the rounds aside. Scrub the mussels with a stiff brush and pull out the hairy beards. Discard any broken mussels, or open ones that don't close when tapped on the bench. Rinse well.

Lightly coat the fish in flour. Heat the oil in a large frying pan and fry the fish in batches over medium heat for 2–3 minutes, or until cooked and golden brown all over. Transfer to a large casserole dish. Add a little oil to the pan if necessary, add the calamari and cook, stirring, for 1–2 minutes. Remove and add to the fish. Cook the lobster rounds and prawns for 2–3 minutes, or until the prawns turn pink, then add to the soup.

Add the wine to the pan and bring to the boil. Reduce the heat, add the mussels, cover and steam for 4–5 minutes. Add to the soup, discarding any unopened mussels. Ensuring nothing flammable is nearby, pour the brandy into one side of the pan and, when it has warmed, carefully ignite the brandy. Gently shake the pan until the flames have died down. Pour this mixture over the seafood in the casserole dish. Pour the sofrito sauce over the top. Cover and bake for 20 minutes. Stir in the picada sauce and cook for a further 10 minutes, or until warmed through — do not overcook or the seafood will toughen. Sprinkle with parsley and serve.

PREPARATION TIME: 40 MINUTES   COOKING TIME: 1 HOUR 10 MINUTES

CHINESE LAMB, GARLIC CHIVE AND CELLOPHANE NOODLE SOUP

2 tablespoons light soy sauce

1 tablespoon oyster sauce

1 tablespoon Chinese rice wine

1 teaspoon sugar

1¼ teaspoons sesame oil

3 slices fresh ginger plus 1 tablespoon finely chopped ginger

250 g (9 oz) lamb fillet

100 g (3½ oz) cellophane noodles

1 tablespoon vegetable oil

2 spring onions (scallions), finely chopped, plus extra, to serve

125 g (4½ oz) chopped garlic chives

1 litre (35 fl oz/4 cups) chicken stock

SERVES 4

Combine the soy sauce, oyster sauce, rice wine, sugar, ¼ teaspoon of the sesame oil and the ginger slices in a bowl. Add the lamb and marinate for 3 hours, turning occasionally. Remove the lamb and ginger from the marinade with tongs. Set aside.

Meanwhile, soak the noodles in a bowl of boiling water for 3–4 minutes. Rinse, drain and set aside.

Heat a wok over high heat, add the vegetable oil and the remaining sesame oil and swirl to coat the base and side. Add the chopped ginger, chopped spring onion and garlic chives and cook for 30 seconds, stirring constantly. Slowly pour in the stock then bring to the boil. Add the lamb and ginger slices, reduce the heat to low, cover with a lid and poach the lamb for 10 minutes.

Remove the lamb from the wok. Bring the soup to the boil over medium heat. Meanwhile, thinly slice the lamb. Return the sliced lamb to the wok and add the noodles at the same time, stirring well until mixed together. Serve hot with the sliced spring onion scattered over the top.

PREPARATION TIME: 10 MINUTES + COOKING TIME: 20 MINUTES

CHICKEN GUMBO

80 ml (2½ fl oz/⅓ cup) vegetable oil
30 g (1 oz/¼ cup) plain (all-purpose) flour
450 g (1 lb) tomatoes
600 g (1 lb 5 oz) boneless, skinless chicken thighs
60 g (2¼ oz) unsalted butter
100 g (3½ oz) smoked ham, diced
150 g (5½ oz) chorizo, thinly sliced
2 onions, chopped
2 garlic cloves, finely chopped
2 celery stalks, thinly sliced
1 red capsicum (pepper), seeded, membrane removed and finely chopped
500 ml (17 fl oz/2 cups) chicken stock
1 bay leaf
2 teaspoons thyme
Tabasco sauce, to taste
350 g (12 oz) okra, cut into 1 cm (½ inch) slices
2 spring onions (scallions), sliced (optional)
2 tablespoons chopped parsley (optional)

SERVES 4–6

Heat 3 tablespoons of the oil in a small, heavy-based saucepan, add the flour and stir to make a smooth paste. Stir over very low heat for 1 hour, or until the roux turns very dark brown, but is not burnt. This requires a great deal of patience and stirring but provides the gumbo with its dark look and rich flavour — when it is done, the roux should be the colour of dark chocolate. Remove from the heat.

Score a cross in the base of each tomato. Put in a heatproof bowl and cover with boiling water. Leave for 30 seconds then transfer to cold water and peel the skin away from the cross. Cut the tomatoes in half, scoop out the seeds and roughly chop the flesh.

Pat the chicken thighs dry with paper towels, cut into quarters and lightly season. Heat the remaining oil and half the butter in a heavy-based frying pan over medium heat. Cook the chicken for about 5 minutes, or until golden brown. Remove the chicken with a slotted spoon. Add the ham and chorizo and cook for 4–5 minutes, or until lightly golden. Remove, leaving as much rendered fat in the pan as possible.

Add the remaining butter to the same pan and cook the onion, garlic, celery and capsicum over medium heat for 5–6 minutes, or until the vegetables have softened but not browned. Transfer the vegetables to a heavy-based, flameproof casserole dish. Add the tomatoes and the roux to the vegetables and stir well. Gradually stir the stock into the pan. Add the herbs and season with the Tabasco. Bring to the boil, stirring constantly. Reduce the heat, add the chicken, ham and chorizo to the casserole dish and simmer, uncovered, for 1 hour. Add the okra and cook for a further hour. Skim the surface as the gumbo cooks because a lot of oil will come out of the chorizo. The gumbo should thicken considerably in the last 20 minutes as the okra softens. Remove the bay leaf and serve. Garnish with spring onion and parsley, if desired.

PREPARATION TIME: 15 MINUTES   COOKING TIME: 2 HOURS 30 MINUTES

NOTE: Gumbo is a speciality of Cajun cuisine and is a cross between a soup and a stew. Traditionally, gumbo is served in deep bowls, each containing a few tablespoons of cooked rice in the bottom.

BEAN SOUP WITH SAUSAGE

4 Italian sausages
2 teaspoons olive oil
2 leeks, white part only, sliced
1 garlic clove, crushed
1 large carrot, chopped into small cubes
2 celery stalks, sliced
2 tablespoons plain (all-purpose) flour
2 beef stock (bouillon) cubes, crumbled
2 litres (70 fl oz/8 cups) boiling water
125 ml (4 fl oz/½ cup) white wine
125 g (4½ oz) conchiglie (shell pasta)
440 g (15½ oz) tinned mixed beans, drained
chopped parsley, to serve (optional)

SERVES 4–6

Cut the sausages into small pieces. Heat the oil in a large heavy-based saucepan and add the sausage pieces. Cook over medium heat for 5 minutes, or until golden, stirring regularly. Remove from the pan, set aside and drain on paper towel.

Add the leek, garlic, carrot and celery to the pan and cook for 2–3 minutes or until soft, stirring occasionally. Add the flour and stir for 1 minute. Gradually stir in the combined stock cubes, water and the wine. Bring to the boil, reduce the heat and simmer for 10 minutes.

Add the pasta and beans to the pan. Increase the heat and cook for 8–10 minutes, or until the pasta is *al dente*. Return the sausage to the pan and season to taste. Serve with chopped fresh parsley, if desired.

PREPARATION TIME: 25 MINUTES   COOKING TIME: 40 MINUTES

NOTE: Use dried beans, if preferred. Put them in a bowl, cover with water and soak overnight. Drain and add to a large saucepan with enough water to cover the beans well. Bring to the boil, reduce the heat and simmer for 1 hour. Drain well before adding to the soup.

BACON AND PEA SOUP

4 bacon slices
50 g (1¾ oz) butter
1 large onion, finely chopped
1 celery stalk, thinly sliced
2 litres (70 fl oz/8 cups) chicken stock
150 g (5½ oz/1 cup) frozen peas
250 g (9 oz) rissoni
2 tablespoons chopped parsley

SERVES 4–6

Trim the rind and excess fat from the bacon and chop into small pieces.

Melt the butter in a large heavy-based saucepan and cook the bacon, onion and celery over low heat for 5 minutes, stirring occasionally. Add the stock and peas and simmer, covered, for 5 minutes. Increase the heat, add the rissoni and cook, uncovered, stirring occasionally, for 5 minutes, or until the rissoni is tender. Add the chopped parsley and season to taste, just before serving.

PREPARATION TIME: 20 MINUTES   COOKING TIME: 15 MINUTES

CHINESE HOT AND SOUR NOODLE SOUP

STOCK

1.5 kg (3 lb 5 oz) chicken bones, washed

2 slices fresh ginger

4 spring onions (scallions), white part only, bruised

200 g (7 oz) fresh Shanghai noodles

200 g (7 oz) boneless, skinless chicken breast, cut into very thin strips

2 tablespoons garlic

2 tablespoons red chilli paste

60 ml (2 fl oz/1/4 cup) light soy sauce

3/4 teaspoon ground white pepper

4 fresh shiitake mushrooms, stems removed, caps thinly sliced

100 g (3½ oz) enoki mushrooms, trimmed and separated

115 g (4 oz) fresh baby corn, cut lengthways

60 ml (2 fl oz/1/4 cup) Chinese black vinegar

60 g (2¼ oz) black fungus, roughly chopped

200 g (7 oz) firm tofu, cut into 2.5 cm (1 inch) cubes

30 g (1 oz/1/4 cup) cornflour (cornstarch)

3 eggs, lightly beaten

1 teaspoon sesame oil

spring onions (scallions), thinly sliced, to garnish

SERVES 6

To make the stock, put the chicken bones and 3.5 litres (122 fl oz) water in a large saucepan and bring to a simmer, but do not boil. Cook for 30 minutes, removing any scum that rises to the surface. Add the ginger and spring onion and simmer gently, partially covered, for 3 hours. Strain through a fine sieve and allow to cool. Cover and refrigerate overnight. Remove the layer of fat from the surface.

Cook the noodles in a large saucepan of boiling water for 4–5 minutes, then drain, rinse and set aside.

To make the soup, pour 2 litres (70 fl oz/4 cups) of the stock into a non-stick wok, bring to the boil over high heat. Reduce the heat to medium, add the chicken, garlic and chilli paste, soy sauce, white pepper and stir well. Simmer, covered, for 10 minutes, or until the chicken is cooked. Add the mushrooms, corn, vinegar, black fungus and tofu. Season with salt, return the lid to the wok and simmer gently for 5 minutes — do not stir.

Mix the cornflour with 60 ml (2 fl oz/1/4 cup) water. Add to the soup with the noodles, return to a simmer then pour the eggs in a very thin stream over the surface. Turn off the heat and stand for 10 minutes before gently stirring in the sesame oil. Divide among the serving bowls and garnish with spring onions.

PREPARATION TIME: 45 MINUTES +   COOKING TIME: 4 HOURS

HARIRA

2 tablespoons olive oil
2 small brown onions, chopped
2 large garlic cloves, crushed
500 g (1 lb 2 oz) lamb shoulder steaks,
trimmed of excess fat and sinew,
and cut into small chunks
1½ teaspoons ground cumin
2 teaspoons paprika
½ teaspoon ground cloves
1 bay leaf
2 tablespoons tomato paste
(concentrated purée)
1 litre (35 fl oz/4 cups) beef stock
900 g (2 lb) tinned chickpeas,
rinsed and drained
800 g (1 lb 12 oz) tinned diced tomatoes
30 g (1 oz) finely chopped coriander
(cilantro) leaves, plus extra, to garnish
small black olives, to serve

SERVES 4

Heat the oil in a large heavy-based saucepan or stockpot, add the onion and garlic and cook for 5 minutes, or until softened. Add the meat, in batches, and cook over high heat until browned on all sides. Return all the meat to the pan.

Add the spices and bay leaf to the pan and cook until fragrant. Add the tomato paste and cook for about 2 minutes, stirring constantly. Add the stock, stir well and bring to the boil. Add the chickpeas, tomato and chopped coriander to the pan. Stir, then bring to the boil. Reduce the heat and simmer for 2 hours, or until the meat is tender. Stir occasionally. Season to taste.

Serve garnished with coriander leaves and small black olives. This dish can also be served with toasted pitta bread drizzled with a little extra virgin olive oil.

PREPARATION TIME: 15 MINUTES   COOKING TIME: 2 HOURS 25 MINUTES

PENANG FISH LAKSA

1 whole snapper (750 g/1 lb 10 oz), scaled and cleaned
750 ml (26 fl oz/3 cups) chicken stock
6 Vietnamese mint stalks
4 dried red chillies
250 ml (9 fl oz/1 cup) boiling water
3 cm (1¼ inch) piece of galangal, finely chopped
4 red Asian shallots, finely chopped
2 lemon grass stems, white part only, finely chopped
1 teaspoon ground turmeric
1 teaspoon shrimp paste
4 tablespoons tamarind purée
1 tablespoon sugar
500 g (1 lb 2 oz) fresh rice noodles
1 small Lebanese (short) cucumber, seeded and cut into strips
3 tablespoons Vietnamese mint
1 large green chilli, sliced

SERVES 4

Trim the fins and tail off the fish with kitchen scissors. Make several deep cuts through the thickest part of the fish on both sides.

Pour the stock and 750 ml (26 fl oz/3 cups) water into a non-stick wok. Add the mint stalks and bring to the boil over high heat. Put the fish in the wok and simmer for 10 minutes, or until cooked. The fish should remain submerged during cooking — you might need to add some more boiling water. Lift the fish out of the wok and allow to cool.

Soak the dried chillies in the boiling water for 20 minutes. Drain and chop. To make the laksa paste, put the chilli, galangal, shallots, lemon grass, turmeric and shrimp paste in a food processor or blender and blend to a smooth paste, adding a little water if needed.

Flake the flesh off the fish and remove all the bones, reserving both. Add the bones and tamarind to the stock in the wok and bring to the boil. Simmer for 10 minutes, then strain and return the liquid to a clean wok — make sure no bones slip through. Stir the laksa paste into the liquid and simmer over medium heat for 10 minutes. Stir in the sugar, add the fish flesh and simmer for 1–2 minutes, or until the fish is heated through.

Put the noodles in a heatproof bowl, cover with boiling water then gently separate. Drain immediately and refresh under cold water. Divide the noodles among four serving bowls. Ladle on the fish pieces and broth then sprinkle with the cucumber, mint and chilli and serve.

PREPARATION TIME: 20 MINUTES +   COOKING TIME: 40 MINUTES

JAPANESE UDON MISO SOUP WITH CHICKEN

8 dried shiitake mushrooms
250 ml (9 fl oz/1 cup) boiling water
400 g (14 oz) fresh udon noodles
1 litre (35 fl oz/4 cups) chicken stock
600 g (1 lb 5 oz) boneless, skinless
chicken breast, cut into 1.5 cm (5/8 inch)
thick strips
300 g (10½ oz) baby bok choy (pak choy),
halved lengthways
60 g (2¼ oz/¼ cup) white miso paste
2 teaspoons dashi granules
1 tablespoon wakame flakes or other
seaweed
150 g (5½ oz) silken firm tofu, cut into
1 cm (½ inch) cubes
3 spring onions (scallions), sliced
diagonally

SERVES 4–6

Soak the mushrooms in the boiling water for 20 minutes. Squeeze dry, reserving the soaking liquid. Discard the woody stalks and thinly slice the caps. Set aside.

Bring 2 litres (70 fl oz/8 cups) water to the boil in a large saucepan and cook the noodles for 1–2 minutes, or until tender. Drain immediately and rinse under cold water. Set aside.

Pour the stock and 1 litre (35 fl oz/4 cups) water into a wok and bring to the boil, then reduce the heat and simmer. Add the chicken and cook for 2–3 minutes, or until almost cooked through.

Add the mushrooms and cook for 1 minute. Add the bok choy halves and simmer for a further minute, or until beginning to wilt, then add the miso paste, dashi granules, wakame and reserved mushroom liquid. Stir to dissolve the dashi and miso paste. Do not allow to boil.

Gently stir in the tofu. Distribute the noodles among the serving bowls then ladle the hot soup over them. Sprinkle with the spring onion.

PREPARATION TIME: 35 MINUTES +   COOKING TIME: 15 MINUTES

LAMB HOTPOT WITH RICE NOODLES

2 garlic cloves, crushed

2 teaspoons grated ginger

1 teaspoon five-spice

¼ teaspoon ground white pepper

2 tablespoons Chinese rice wine

1 teaspoon sugar

1 kg (2 lb 4 oz) boneless lamb shoulder, trimmed and cut into 3 cm (1¼ inch) pieces

30 g (1 oz) dried Chinese mushrooms

1 tablespoon peanut oil

1 large onion, cut into wedges

2 cm (¾ inch) piece of ginger, cut into thin strips

1 teaspoon sichuan peppercorns, crushed

2 tablespoons sweet bean paste

1 teaspoon black peppercorns, ground and toasted

500 ml (17 fl oz/2 cups) chicken stock

60 ml (2 fl oz/¼ cup) oyster sauce

2 star anise

60 ml (2 fl oz/¼ cup) Chinese rice wine, extra

80 g (2¾ oz) tinned sliced bamboo shoots, drained

100 g (3½ oz) tinned water chestnuts, drained and sliced

400 g (14 oz) fresh rice noodles, cut into 2 cm (¾ inch) wide strips

1 spring onion (scallion), sliced, to serve

SERVES 4

Combine the garlic, grated ginger, five-spice, white pepper, rice wine, sugar and 1 teaspoon salt in a large bowl. Add the lamb and toss to coat. Cover and marinate for 2 hours.

Meanwhile, soak the dried mushrooms in boiling water for 30 minutes then drain and squeeze out any excess water. Remove and discard the stems. Chop the caps.

Heat a wok over high heat, add the oil and swirl to coat the base and side. Stir-fry the onion, ginger strips and sichuan peppercorns for 2 minutes. Add the lamb in batches and cook for 2–3 minutes, or until starting to brown. Return all the lamb to the wok. Stir in the bean paste and ground peppercorns and cook for 3 minutes. Transfer to a 2 litre (70 fl oz/8 cup) flameproof clay pot or casserole dish. Stir in the stock, oyster sauce, star anise and extra rice wine and simmer, covered, over low heat for 1½ hours, or until the lamb is tender. Stir in the bamboo shoots and water chestnuts and cook for 20 minutes. Add the mushrooms.

Cover the noodles with boiling water and gently separate. Drain and rinse, then add to the hotpot, stirring for 1–2 minutes, or until heated through. Sprinkle with spring onion to serve.

PREPARATION TIME: 20 MINUTES +   COOKING TIME: 2 HOURS

CALDO VERDE

150 g (5½ oz) chorizo sausage, thinly sliced
2 tablespoons olive oil
1 large onion, thinly sliced
4 garlic cloves, finely chopped
2 teaspoons finely chopped oregano
1 large potato, peeled and diced
200 g (7 oz/1 cup) long-grain rice
1 litre (35 fl oz/4 cups) chicken stock
1 small green chilli, split lengthways
270 g (9½ oz) finely shredded kale, silverbeet (Swiss chard) or English spinach
1 large handful flat leaf (Italian) parsley, chopped
extra virgin olive oil, for drizzling
lemon wedges, to serve

SERVES 6

Fry the chorizo in a frying pan over medium heat for 5 minutes, or until slightly crispy. Set aside.

Heat the olive oil in a large saucepan then add the onion, garlic and oregano and cook over medium heat for 8 minutes, or until the onion is softened but not browned. Add the potato and rice and cook for a further 5 minutes, stirring to make sure it doesn't catch on the bottom of the pan.

Pour in the stock, 1 litre (35 fl oz/4 cups) water and the chilli, increase the heat and bring to the boil, stirring occasionally. Reduce the heat and simmer for about 20 minutes, or until the rice is tender and the potato is starting to fall apart, skimming as needed. Discard the chilli. Lightly crush the potato with a vegetable masher then add the kale and chorizo. Cook for a further 15 minutes, or until the kale is softened and loses its raw flavour.

Stir in the chopped parsley and season to taste. Ladle into bowls and drizzle with extra virgin olive oil, if desired. Serve with lemon wedges to squeeze over the top.

PREPARATION TIME: 15 MINUTES   COOKING TIME: 1 HOUR

NOTE: Originating in the northern Portuguese province of Minho, this hearty soup is popular throughout the country. The authentic recipe calls for *couve tronchuda*, a dark green cabbage, and *linguiça*, a spicy Portuguese sausage; however, as both are difficult to obtain outside the Iberian peninsula, we have used kale and chorizo instead.

SPANISH-STYLE RICE, MUSSEL, PRAWN AND CHORIZO SOUP

500 g (1 lb 2 oz) raw prawns (shrimp)
1 kg (2 lb 4 oz) black mussels
250 ml (9 fl oz/1 cup) dry sherry
1 tablespoon olive oil
1 red onion, chopped
200 g (7 oz) chorizo sausage, thinly sliced
4 garlic cloves, crushed
100 g (3½ oz/½ cup) long-grain rice
400 g (14 oz) tinned chopped tomatoes
2 litres (70 fl oz/8 cups) chicken stock
½ teaspoon saffron threads
2 bay leaves
1 tablespoon chopped oregano
3 tablespoons chopped flat-leaf (Italian) parsley

SERVES 4

Peel the prawns, leaving the tails intact. Gently pull out the dark vein from each prawn back, starting from the head end. Scrub the mussels with a stiff brush and pull out the hairy beards. Discard any broken mussels or open ones that don't close when tapped on the bench. Rinse well.

Put the mussels in a saucepan with the sherry and cook, covered, over high heat for 3 minutes, or until the mussels have opened. Strain the liquid into a bowl. Discard any unopened mussels. Remove all but eight mussels from their shells and discard the empty shells.

Heat the oil in a large saucepan over medium heat, add the onion and cook for 5 minutes, or until softened but not browned. Add the chorizo and cook for 3–5 minutes, or until browned then add the garlic and cook for a further 1 minute. Add the rice and stir to coat with the chorizo mixture. Add the reserved cooking liquid and cook for 1 minute before adding the chopped tomatoes, stock, saffron, bay leaves and oregano. Bring to the boil then reduce the heat and simmer, covered, for 25 minutes.

Add the prawns and the mussels (except the ones in their shells) to the soup, cover with a lid, and cook for 3 minutes then stir in the parsley. Ladle into four serving bowls, then top each bowl with two mussels still in their shells.

PREPARATION TIME: 45 MINUTES   COOKING TIME: 45 MINUTES

CHORBA BIL HOUT

2 red capsicums (peppers), quartered,
seeded and membrane removed

1 long fresh red chilli, seeded

2 tablespoons extra virgin olive oil

1 brown onion, finely chopped

1 tablespoon tomato paste (concentrated purée)

2–3 teaspoons harissa

4 garlic cloves, finely chopped

2 teaspoons ground cumin

750 ml (26 fl oz/3 cups) fish stock

400 g (14 oz) tinned crushed tomatoes

750 g (1 lb 10 oz) skinless firm white fish
fillets, such as blue eye or ling,
cut into 2 cm (³/4 inch) squares

2 bay leaves

2 tablespoons chopped coriander
(cilantro) leaves

6 thick slices baguette

1 garlic clove, extra, halved

Grill (broil) the capsicum and chilli until the skin is blackened and blistered. Cool in a plastic bag then peel and cut into thin strips.

Heat the oil in a large saucepan and cook the onion for 5 minutes, or until softened. Add the tomato paste, harissa, garlic, cumin and 125 ml (4 fl oz/½ cup) water then stir to combine. Add the fish stock, tomatoes and 500 ml (17 fl oz/2 cups) water. Bring to the boil, then reduce the heat and add the fish and bay leaves. Simmer for 3–5 minutes, or until the fish is just cooked. Remove the fish with a slotted spoon and place on a plate. Discard the bay leaves. When the soup has cooled slightly, add half the chopped coriander and purée in batches, in a food processor, until smooth. Season to taste.

Return the soup to the pan, add the fish, capsicum and chilli and simmer gently while you prepare the toasts.

Toast the bread and, while still warm, rub with the cut garlic. Place one slice of bread in each soup bowl and pile several pieces of fish on top. Ladle the soup over the top, distributing the capsicum evenly. Garnish with the remaining coriander.

SERVES 6   PREPARATION TIME: 30 MINUTES   COOKING TIME: 30 MINUTES

SPICY VIETNAMESE BEEF AND PORK NOODLE SOUP

300 g (10½ oz) beef fillet steak
¼ cup (60 ml/2 fl oz) vegetable oil
300 g (10½ oz) pork leg fillet, cut into
3 cm (1¼ inch) cubes
1 large onion, cut into thin wedges
2 litres (70 fl oz/8 cups) beef stock
2 lemon grass stems
2 tablespoons fish sauce
1 teaspoon ground dried shrimp
1 teaspoon sugar
2 large red chillies, sliced
400 g (14 oz) fresh rice noodles
185 g (6½ oz/2 cups) bean sprouts,
trimmed
3 tablespoons mint
15 g (½ oz) coriander (cilantro) leaves
thinly sliced chilli, to serve (optional)

SERVES 4

Put the beef in the freezer for 20–30 minutes, or until partially frozen then cut into paper-thin slices across the grain. Set aside.

Heat a wok until hot, add 1 tablespoon of the oil and swirl to coat the base and side. Stir-fry the pork in batches for 2–3 minutes, or until browned. Remove from the wok and set aside.

Add another tablespoon of oil and stir-fry the onion for 2–3 minutes, or until softened. Pour in the stock and 500 ml (17 fl oz/2 cups) water. Bruise one of the lemon grass stems and add it to the wok. Return the pork to the wok and bring the liquid to the boil, then reduce the heat and simmer for 15 minutes, or until the pork is tender, periodically skimming off any scum that rises to the surface. Meanwhile, thinly slice the white part of the remaining lemon grass stem.

Remove the whole lemon grass stem from the broth and stir in the fish sauce, dried shrimp and sugar and keep at a simmer.

Heat the remaining oil in a small frying pan over medium heat and cook the sliced lemon grass and chilli for 2–3 minutes, or until fragrant. Stir into the broth. Just before serving, bring the broth to the boil over medium–high heat.

Meanwhile, put the rice noodles in a large heatproof bowl, cover with boiling water and gently separate the noodles. Drain immediately and rinse. Divide the noodles among four warm serving bowls. Top with the bean sprouts and cover with the boiling broth. Add the beef to the soup — the heat of the soup will cook it. Sprinkle with the mint, coriander, and chilli, if desired. Serve immediately.

PREPARATION TIME: 20 MINUTES +   COOKING TIME: 40 MINUTES

INDONESIAN SPICY CHICKEN SOUP

2 teaspoons coriander seeds
2 tablespoons vegetable oil
1.4 kg (3 lb 2 oz) whole chicken, jointed into 8 pieces
4 garlic cloves
1 onion, chopped
2 teaspoons finely sliced ginger
1 dried red chilli, halved
2 lemon grass stems, white part only, roughly chopped
50 g (1¾ oz) coriander (cilantro) roots and stems, well rinsed, roughly chopped
2 teaspoons ground turmeric
1 teaspoon galangal powder
1 teaspoon sugar
1 teaspoon ground coriander
1 litre (35 fl oz/4 cups) chicken stock
2 tablespoons lemon juice
120 g (4¼ oz) cellophane noodles
1½ tablespoons fish sauce
90 g (3¼ oz/1 cup) bean sprouts, trimmed
3 tablespoons chopped coriander (cilantro) leaves
4 spring onions (scallions), thinly sliced
20 g (¾ oz/¼ cup) crisp fried onions
1 tablespoon sambal oelek

SERVES 6

Dry-fry the coriander seeds in a small frying pan over medium heat for 1 minute, or until fragrant. Cool, then finely grind using a mortar and pestle.

Heat a wok to very hot, add 2 teaspoons of the oil and swirl to coat the base and side. Add the chicken pieces and cook in batches for 3–4 minutes, or until browned all over. Remove from the wok and set aside.

Heat the remaining oil in the wok then add the garlic, onion, ginger and chilli and stir-fry for 5 minutes, or until softened. Add the lemon grass, coriander root and stem, turmeric, galangal, sugar and ground coriander and cook for 5 minutes. Return the chicken to the wok and pour in the stock, lemon juice and 500 ml (17 fl oz/2 cups) water to cover the chicken. Cover the wok with a lid and simmer for 20 minutes, skimming the surface periodically to remove any scum that rises to the surface. Remove only the chicken breast pieces, then cover the wok and simmer (still skimming the surface occasionally) for 20 minutes before removing the rest of the chicken pieces. Cover and refrigerate the chicken until needed. Return the lid to the wok and simmer the broth over low heat for 1 hour. Strain through a fine sieve, and allow to cool to room temperature before covering with plastic wrap and refrigerating overnight.

Soak the cellophane noodles in boiling water for 3–4 minutes then drain and rinse.

Remove any fat from the top of the cold broth. Remove the flesh from the chicken and shred with a fork. Place the broth and chicken flesh in the wok, and place over medium heat. Bring to the boil, then stir in the fish sauce, bean sprouts, coriander leaves and noodles. Season well, then ladle into large bowls. Sprinkle with spring onion and crisp fried onion, and serve with sambal oelek.

PREPARATION TIME: OVERNIGHT + 30 MINUTES +   COOKING TIME: 2 HOURS

TWELVE VARIETIES SOUP

300 g (10½ oz) pork liver or lamb liver
200 g (7 oz) boneless, skinless chicken breast
30 g (1 oz) dried Chinese mushrooms
60 ml (2 fl oz/¼ cup) oil
3 onions, finely sliced
4 garlic cloves, finely chopped
1 teaspoon finely chopped fresh ginger
2 tablespoons fish sauce
40 g (1½ oz/⅓ cup) green beans, sliced
40 g (1½ oz/⅓ cup) small cauliflower florets
30 g (1 oz/⅓ cup) sliced button mushrooms
15 g (½ oz/⅓ cup) shredded Chinese cabbage (wong bok)
20 g (¾ oz/⅓ cup) shredded spinach
30 g (1 oz/⅓ cup) bean sprouts, trimmed
3 spring onions (scallions), finely sliced
1 tablespoon coriander (cilantro) leaves
3 eggs
1 tablespoon soy sauce
lime wedges, to serve

SERVES 8

Cook the liver in simmering water for 5 minutes. Remove from heat, allow to cool and slice thinly. Cut the chicken into thin slices. Put the Chinese mushrooms in a heatproof bowl, cover with boiling water and soak for 20 minutes. Drain well and slice.

Heat the oil in a wok, add the onion and cook over medium heat for 5 minutes, or until golden. Add the slices of liver and chicken and stir to combine. Add the garlic and ginger and cook for 1 minute, then pour in the fish sauce and cook for a further 2 minutes.

Put the Chinese mushrooms, beans, cauliflower, button mushrooms and onion mixture in a large saucepan. Add 2 litres (70 fl oz/8 cups) water, bring to the boil and cook until the vegetables are just tender. Add the cabbage, spinach and bean sprouts and cook a further 5 minutes, or until just tender. Stir in the spring onion and coriander.

Break the eggs into the boiling soup and stir immediately. (The eggs will break up and cook.) Add the soy sauce and ¼ teaspoon ground black pepper. Serve immediately with the lime wedges to squeeze into the soup.

PREPARATION TIME: 45 MINUTES + COOKING TIME: 20 MINUTES

PIE-CRUST MUSHROOM SOUP

400 g (14 oz) large field mushrooms
60 g (2¼ oz) butter
1 onion, finely chopped
1 garlic clove, crushed
30 g (1 oz/¼ cup) plain (all-purpose) flour
750 ml (26 fl oz/3 cups) chicken stock
2 tablespoons thyme leaves
2 tablespoons sherry
250 ml (9 fl oz/1 cup) pouring (whipping) cream
1 sheet frozen puff pastry, thawed
1 egg, lightly beaten

SERVES 4

Preheat the oven to 200°C (400°F/Gas 6). Peel and roughly chop the mushrooms, including the stems.

Melt the butter in a large saucepan, add the onion and cook over medium heat for 3 minutes, or until soft. Add the garlic and cook for 1 minute. Add the mushrooms and cook until soft. Sprinkle with the flour and stir for 1 minute. Stir in the stock and thyme and bring to the boil. Reduce the heat and simmer, covered, for 15 minutes. Allow to cool slightly before transferring to a food processor and blending, in batches.

Return the soup to the pan, stir in the sherry and cream then pour into four ovenproof bowls (use small, deep bowls rather than wide shallow ones, or the pastry may sag into the soup).

Cut rounds of pastry slightly larger than the bowl tops and cover each bowl with pastry. Seal the pastry edges and brush lightly with the egg. Place the bowls on a baking tray and bake for 15 minutes, or until golden and puffed.

PREPARATION TIME: 25 MINUTES   COOKING TIME: 35 MINUTES

VIETNAMESE COMBINATION SEAFOOD SOUP

400 g (14 oz) black mussels
500 g (1 lb 2 oz) raw prawns (shrimp)
1 tablespoon vegetable oil
1 lemon grass stem, white part only, finely chopped
1 red chilli, finely chopped
2 garlic cloves, finely chopped
1.5 litres (52 fl oz/6 cups) chicken stock diluted with 500 ml (17 fl oz/2 cups) water
1 tablespoon tamarind purée
1 tablespoon fish sauce
500 g (1 lb 2 oz) firm white fish fillets, such as ling, blue eye or snapper, cut into 2.5 cm (1 inch) pieces
1 ripe tomato, cut into thin wedges
3 tablespoons fresh coriander leaves
1 tablespoon fresh Vietnamese mint
90 g (3 oz/1 cup) bean sprouts, trimmed

Scrub the mussels with a stiff brush and pull out the hairy beards. Discard any broken mussels, or open ones that don't close when tapped on the bench. Rinse well. Peel the prawns, leaving the tails intact. Gently pull out the dark vein from each prawn back, starting from the head end.

Heat a non-stick wok over high heat, add the oil and swirl to coat the base and side. Add the lemon grass, chilli and garlic, then cook for 2 minutes, or until softened and fragrant. Add the stock, tamarind and fish sauce, bring to the boil, then reduce the heat to low and simmer for 15 minutes.

Increase the heat to medium–high, add the mussels, cover with a lid and cook for 2–3 minutes, tossing occasionally. Remove the lid and add the prawns, fish pieces and tomato wedges. Cook for a further 3 minutes, or until the seafood is completely cooked. Discard any unopened mussels. Stir in the coriander leaves and mint.

Divide the bean sprouts among four soup bowls, ladle in the soup and serve immediately.

SERVES 4   PREPARATION TIME: 30 MINUTES   COOKING TIME: 30 MINUTES

NOTE: It is important to use a non-stick or stainless steel wok for this recipe, as the tamarind purée reacts with a regular wok and will taint the whole dish.

RAINBOW CONGEE

200 g (7 oz) short-grain rice
2 dried Chinese mushrooms
85 g (3 oz) snow peas (mangetout), trimmed
2 Chinese sausages (lap cheong)
2 tablespoons oil
¼ red onion, finely diced
1 carrot, cut into 1 cm (½ inch) cubes
3 teaspoons light soy sauce
2 litres (70 fl oz/8 cups) chicken stock

SERVES 6

Put the rice in a bowl and, using your fingers as a rake, rinse under cold running water to remove any dust. Drain the rice in a colander. Soak the dried mushrooms in boiling water for 30 minutes then drain and squeeze out any excess water. Remove and discard the stems and chop the caps into 5 mm (¼ inch) cubes. Cut the snow peas into 1 cm (½ inch) pieces.

Place the sausages on a plate in a steamer. Cover and steam over simmering water in a wok for 10 minutes, then cut them into 1 cm (½ inch) pieces.

Heat the oil in a wok over medium heat. Stir-fry the sausage until it is brown and the fat has melted out of it. Remove with a wire sieve or slotted spoon and drain. Pour the oil from the wok, leaving 1 tablespoon.

Reheat the reserved oil over high heat until very hot. Stir-fry the red onion until soft and transparent. Add the mushrooms and carrot and stir-fry for 1 minute, or until fragrant.

Put the mushroom mixture in a clay pot, casserole dish or saucepan and stir in the soy sauce, rice, chicken stock and ¼ teaspoon salt. Bring to the boil, then reduce the heat and simmer very gently, stirring occasionally, for 1¾–2 hours, or until it has a porridge-like texture and the rice is breaking up. If it is too thick, add some water and return to the boil. Toss in the snow peas and sausage, cover and stand for 5 minutes before serving.

PREPARATION TIME: 15 MINUTES +   COOKING TIME: 2 HOURS 15 MINUTES

CLEAR CHINESE PORK BALL AND NOODLE SOUP

1 tablespoon peanut oil

2 teaspoons sesame oil

4 garlic cloves, crushed

2 teaspoons grated fresh ginger

150 g (5½ oz) Chinese cabbage (wong bok), shredded

300 g (10½ oz) minced (ground) pork

1 egg white

1½ tablespoons cornflour (cornstarch)

¼ teaspoon ground white pepper

80 ml (2½ fl oz/⅓ cup) light soy sauce

2 tablespoons Chinese rice wine

6 spring onions (scallions), thinly sliced

15 g (½ oz) coriander (cilantro) leaves, finely chopped

1.25 litres (44 fl oz/5 cups) chicken stock diluted with 250 ml (9 fl oz/1 cup) water

3 teaspoons grated fresh ginger, extra

200 g (7 oz) fresh thin egg noodles

finely chopped red chilli, to garnish (optional)

soy sauce, extra, to serve

SERVES 4–6

Heat a wok over high heat, add the peanut oil and 1 teaspoon of the sesame oil, then swirl to coat the base and side. Add the garlic, ginger and Chinese cabbage and stir-fry for 1 minute, or until the garlic begins to brown. As soon as this happens, remove the wok from the heat and allow to cool.

Transfer the cooled cabbage mixture to a large bowl and add the pork, egg white, cornflour, white pepper, 2 tablespoons of the soy sauce, 1 tablespoon of the rice wine, half the spring onion and 3 tablespoons of the coriander. Mix thoroughly, then cover with plastic wrap and refrigerate for 1 hour. Shape 1 tablespoon of the mixture into a ball using wet hands. Repeat with the remaining mixture.

Pour the stock into a clean wok. Bring to the boil then reduce the heat and simmer for 1–2 minutes. Add the extra ginger, remaining soy sauce and rice wine and cook, covered, for 5 minutes. Add the pork balls. Cook, uncovered, for a further 8–10 minutes, or until the balls rise to the top and are cooked through.

Meanwhile, cook the noodles in a large saucepan of boiling water for 1 minute, or until they separate. Drain then rinse well. Divide the noodles among serving bowls then ladle on the soup. Sprinkle with the remaining spring onion and coriander then add a couple of drops of the remaining sesame oil. Serve with chilli and extra soy sauce, if desired.

PREPARATION TIME: 20 MINUTES + COOKING TIME: 30 MINUTES

LAMB AND FUSILLI SOUP

2 tablespoons oil
500 g (1 lb 2 oz) lean lamb meat, cubed
2 onions, finely chopped
2 carrots, diced
4 celery stalks, diced
425 g (15 oz) tinned crushed tomatoes
2 litres (70 fl oz/8 cups) beef stock
500 g (1 lb 2 oz) fusilli
chopped flat-leaf (Italian) parsley,
to serve

SERVES 6–8

Heat the oil in a large saucepan and cook the cubed lamb, in batches, until golden brown. Remove each batch as it is done and drain on paper towel. Set aside.

Add the onion to the pan and cook for 2 minutes or until softened. Return the meat to the pan, add the carrot, celery, tomato and beef stock. Stir to combine and bring to the boil. Reduce the heat to low and simmer, covered, for 15 minutes. Add the fusilli and stir to prevent the pasta from sticking to the pan. Simmer, uncovered, for a further 10 minutes, or until the lamb and pasta are tender. Sprinkle with parsley before serving.

PREPARATION TIME: 25 MINUTES   COOKING TIME: 40 MINUTES

MINESTRONE SOUP WITH RICE

225 g (8 oz) dried borlotti (cranberry)
beans
55 g (2 oz) butter
1 onion, finely chopped
1 garlic clove, finely chopped
3 tablespoons finely chopped parsley
2 sage leaves
100 g (3½ oz) pancetta, cubed
2 celery stalks, halved, then sliced
2 carrots, sliced
3 potatoes, peeled
1 teaspoon tomato paste (concentrated
purée)
400 g (14 oz) tinned chopped tomatoes
8 basil leaves
3 litres (105 fl oz/12 cups) chicken or
vegetable stock
2 zucchini (courgettes), sliced
225 g (8 oz) fresh peas
125 g (4½ oz) green beans, cut into 4 cm
(1½ inch) lengths
¼ cabbage, shredded
220 g (7¾ oz/1 cup) risotto rice
freshly grated parmesan cheese, to serve

SERVES 6

Put the dried beans in a large bowl, cover with cold water and soak overnight. Drain and rinse under cold water.

Melt the butter in a saucepan and add the onion, garlic, parsley, sage and pancetta. Cook over low heat, stirring once or twice, for 10 minutes, or until the onion is softened but not browned. Add the celery, carrot and potatoes, and cook for 5 minutes. Stir in the tomato paste, chopped tomatoes, basil and borlotti beans. Season with freshly ground black pepper. Pour in the stock and bring slowly to the boil. Cover and leave to simmer for 2 hours, stirring once or twice.

If the potatoes have not broken up by the end of the 2 hours, roughly break them with a fork against the side of the pan. Season to taste then add the zucchini, peas, green beans, cabbage and rice. Simmer for a further 15–20 minutes, or until the rice is cooked. Divide among six soup bowls and sprinkle with a little parmesan cheese, to serve.

PREPARATION TIME: 20 MINUTES +   COOKING TIME: 2 HOURS 30 MINUTES

MANHATTAN-STYLE SEAFOOD CHOWDER

12 large raw prawns (shrimp)
60 g (2¼ oz) butter
3 bacon slices, chopped
2 onions, chopped
2 garlic cloves, finely chopped
2 celery stalks, sliced
3 potatoes, diced
1.25 litres (44 fl oz/5 cups) fish or chicken stock
3 teaspoons chopped thyme
1 tablespoon tomato paste (concentrated purée)
425 g (15 oz) tinned chopped tomatoes
375 g (13 oz) skinless firm white fish fillets such as ling, cod, flake or hake, cut into bite-sized pieces
310 g (11 oz) tinned baby clams (vongole), with liquid
2 tablespoons chopped parsley
grated orange zest, to garnish

SERVES 4–6

Peel the prawns and gently pull out the dark vein from each prawn back, starting at the head end.

Melt the butter in a large saucepan and cook the bacon, onion, garlic and celery over low heat, stirring occasionally, for 5 minutes, or until soft but not brown. Add the potato, stock and thyme and bring to the boil. Reduce the heat and simmer, covered, for 15 minutes. Add the tomato paste and tomato to the pan, stir through and bring back to the boil. Add the fish pieces, prawns and clams with juice and simmer over low heat for 3 minutes.

Just before serving, season to taste and stir in the parsley. Garnish with grated orange zest.

PREPARATION TIME: 30 MINUTES   COOKING TIME: 30 MINUTES

MONGOLIAN HOTPOT

80 ml (2½ fl oz/⅓ cup) light soy sauce
2 tablespoons Chinese sesame paste
3 tablespoons Chinese rice wine
1 teaspoon chilli
1 teaspoon garlic paste
250 g (9 oz) dried rice vermicelli
600 g (1 lb 5 oz) lamb backstraps or loin
fillet, thinly sliced across the grain
4 spring onions (scallions), sliced
1.5 litres (52 fl oz/6 cups) chicken stock
6 thin slices of fresh ginger
300 g (10½ oz) silken firm tofu, cut into
1.5 cm (5/8 inch) cubes
300 g (10½ oz) Chinese broccoli (gai larn),
cut into 4 cm (1½ inch) lengths
90 g (3¼ oz/2 cups) shredded Chinese
cabbage (wong bok)

SERVES 6

To make the sauce, combine the soy sauce, sesame paste, 1 tablespoon rice wine, chilli paste and garlic paste in a small bowl.

Put the vermicelli in a large heatproof bowl, cover with boiling water and soak for 6–7 minutes. Drain well and divide among six serving bowls. Top with the lamb slices and spring onion.

Put the stock, ginger and remaining rice wine in a flameproof hotpot or large saucepan. Cover and bring to the boil over high heat. Add the tofu, Chinese broccoli and Chinese cabbage and simmer, uncovered, for 1 minute, or until the broccoli has wilted. Divide the tofu, broccoli and cabbage among the serving bowls then ladle on the hot stock — it should be hot enough to cook the lamb. Drizzle a little of the sauce on top and serve the rest on the side.

PREPARATION TIME: 15 MINUTES +   COOKING TIME: 5 MINUTES

NOTE: This recipe traditionally uses a Chinese steamboat — this is an aluminium pot with a steam spout in the middle, placed on a propane burner in the middle of the dining table. You could also use a fondue pot.

RAMEN NOODLE SOUP WITH BARBECUED PORK AND GREENS

15 g (½ oz) dried shiitake mushrooms
125 ml (4 fl oz/½ cup) boiling water
350 g (12 oz) Chinese broccoli (gai larn),
trimmed and cut into 4 cm (1½ inch)
lengths
375 g (13 oz) fresh ramen noodles
1.25 litres (44 fl oz/5 cups) chicken stock
diluted with 250 ml (9 fl oz/1 cup) water
60 ml (2 fl oz/¼ cup) soy sauce
1 teaspoon sugar
200 g (7 oz) Chinese barbecued pork
(char siu), thinly sliced
chilli flakes (optional)

SERVES 4

Soak the mushrooms in the boiling water for 20 minutes. Squeeze the mushrooms dry, reserving the liquid. Discard the stalks, then thinly slice the caps. Set aside.

Blanch the Chinese broccoli in a large saucepan of boiling salted water for 3 minutes, or until tender but firm to the bite. Drain, then refresh in cold water. Set aside.

Cook the noodles in a large saucepan of boiling water for 2 minutes, or until just tender. Drain, rinse under cold water then drain again. Set aside.

Pour the stock and 500 ml (17 fl oz/2 cups) water into a non-stick wok and bring to the boil. Add the sliced mushrooms and reserved mushroom liquid, soy sauce and sugar. Simmer for 2 minutes then add the broccoli.

Divide the noodles among four serving bowls. Ladle on the hot stock and vegetables. Top with the pork and chilli flakes, if desired.

PREPARATION TIME: 15 MINUTES +   COOKING TIME: 10 MINUTES

PRAWN AND OKRA GUMBO

PRAWN STOCK

1 kg (2 lb 4 oz) raw prawns (shrimp)
1 tablespoon olive oil
1 onion, chopped
1 carrot, chopped
1 celery stalk, chopped
1 bay leaf
2 whole cloves
3 garlic cloves, bruised
3 parsley stalks
1 thyme sprig
½ teaspoon black peppercorns

2 tablespoons olive oil
500 g (1 lb 2 oz) okra, thickly sliced
200 g (7 oz) chorizo, sliced
250 g (9 oz) smoked ham, diced
60 ml (2 fl oz/¼ cup) olive oil, extra
30 g (1 oz/¼ cup) plain (all-purpose) flour
2 onions, chopped
2 celery stalks, diced
1 red capsicum (pepper), diced
6 garlic cloves, finely chopped
½ teaspoon cayenne pepper
2 teaspoons sweet paprika
2 teaspoons mustard powder
large pinch ground allspice
400 g (14 oz) tomato passata
(puréed tomatoes)
1 tablespoon tomato paste
(concentrated purée)
2 teaspoons finely chopped thyme
2 teaspoons finely chopped oregano
2 bay leaves
2½ tablespoons worcestershire sauce
500 g (1 lb 2 oz) scallops without roe
12 oysters
chopped flat-leaf (Italian) parsley, to serve
cooked long-grain rice, to serve

SERVES 8

To make the stock, peel the prawns, reserving the shells. Gently pull out the dark vein from each prawn back, starting at the head end. Cover the prawn meat and refrigerate until ready to use. Heat the oil in a large saucepan, add the prawn shells and cook over high heat for 8 minutes, or until bright orange. Add 2.5 litres (87 fl oz/10 cups) cold water and the remaining stock ingredients and bring to the boil. Reduce the heat to low and simmer for 30 minutes, skimming occasionally, then strain well and set aside — you should have about 2 litres (70 fl oz/8 cups) stock.

Meanwhile, heat the olive oil in a frying pan and sauté the okra over medium heat for 10 minutes, or until slightly softened. Remove from the pan and set aside. Add the chorizo to the pan and cook for 5 minutes, or until well browned, then set aside. Add the ham and cook for a few minutes, or until lightly browned.

Heat the extra olive oil in a large saucepan, add the flour and stir to combine. Cook, stirring regularly over medium heat for 30 seconds, or until the roux turns a colour somewhere between milk and dark chocolate, but do not allow to burn. Add the onion, celery, capsicum and garlic to the roux and cook for about 10 minutes, or until softened. Add the cayenne, paprika, mustard and allspice and stir for 1 minute. Add the tomato passata, tomato paste, prawn stock, thyme, oregano, bay leaves, worcestershire sauce, chorizo and ham and bring to the boil. Reduce the heat to low and simmer for 1 hour then add the okra and continue cooking for a further 1 hour or until the gumbo is thick and glossy.

Add the prawns, scallops and oysters and cook for about 5-8 minutes, or until all the seafood is cooked through. Stir in the parsley and season to taste. Ladle the soup over the hot rice in individual bowls and serve with lemon wedges, if you like.

PREPARATION TIME: 35 MINUTES   COOKING TIME: 3 HOURS

CHINESE LONG AND SHORT NOODLE SOUP

300 g (10½ oz) minced (ground) pork

4 spring onions (scallions), sliced

3 garlic cloves, roughly chopped

2 teaspoons grated fresh ginger

2 teaspoons cornflour (cornstarch)

100 ml (3½ fl oz) light soy sauce

60 ml (2 fl oz/¼ cup) Chinese rice wine

30 won ton wrappers

2.25 litres (80 fl oz/9 cups) chicken stock diluted with 750 ml (26 fl oz/3 cups) water

20 g (¾ oz) fresh ginger, thinly sliced

200 g (7 oz) dried flat egg noodles

2 spring onions (scallions), sliced, extra

1 teaspoon sesame oil

SERVES 6

Put the pork, spring onion, garlic, ginger, cornflour, 1½ tablespoons of the soy sauce and 1 tablespoon of the rice wine in a food processor and process until well combined.

Place 2 teaspoons of the mixture in the centre of a won ton wrapper and lightly brush the edges with water. Lift the sides up tightly and pinch around the filling to form a pouch. Repeat with the remaining filling and wrappers until all the filling is used.

Pour the chicken stock into a large wok, add the ginger and bring to a simmer over medium-high heat. Stir in the remaining soy sauce and wine.

Meanwhile, bring a large saucepan of water to the boil. Reduce the heat, add the won tons and simmer for 1 minute, or until they float to the surface and are cooked through. Remove the won tons with a slotted spoon and set aside. Return the water to the boil, add the egg noodles and cook for 3 minutes, or until just tender. Drain and rinse. Remove the ginger slices from the broth with a slotted spoon, then add the won tons and simmer for 2 minutes, or until they float to the top and are heated through. Add the noodles to the soup to reheat.

Divide the soup and won tons among six large serving bowls, sprinkle with extra spring onion and drizzle each with sesame oil, to taste.

PREPARATION TIME: 30 MINUTES   COOKING TIME. 15 MINUTES

PRAWN AND UDON NOODLE SOUP

500 g (1 lb 2 oz) raw prawns (shrimp)
1½ tablespoons oil
1 lemon grass stem, white part only, chopped
2 garlic cloves, chopped
2 small red chillies, cut in half
2 makrut (kaffir lime) leaves
1 lime, quartered
4 spring onions (scallions), sliced
500 g (1 lb 2 oz) dried udon noodles
2 tablespoons soy sauce
100 g (3½ oz) shiitake mushrooms, halved
1 tablespoon coriander (cilantro) leaves
500 g (1 lb 2 oz) baby bok choy (pak choy), trimmed, leaves separated
lime wedges, extra, to serve

SERVES 6

Peel the prawns, reserving the heads and shells. Gently pull out the dark vein from each prawn back, starting at the head end.

Heat the oil in a large saucepan, add the prawn heads and shells and cook over high heat until pink. Add the lemon grass, garlic, red chillies, lime leaves, lime quarters, half the spring onion and 2 litres (70 fl oz/ 8 cups) water. Bring to the boil, reduce the heat and simmer for 20 minutes. Pour through a fine strainer into a bowl and discard the solids. Rinse the pan and return the stock to the pan.

Add the noodles to a large saucepan of boiling salted water and cook for 5 minutes, or until tender. Drain well.

Bring the stock to the boil. Add the soy sauce and prawns to the pan and cook for 5 minutes, or until the prawns turn pink and are cooked through. Add the remaining ingredients and season to taste.

Divide the cooked noodles among six soup bowls. Ladle the soup over the noodles. The soup can be served garnished with extra lime wedges, if desired.

PREPARATION TIME: 20 MINUTES   COOKING TIME: 30 MINUTES

CANNELLINI BEAN SOUP

500 g (1 lb 2 oz) dried cannellini beans

450 g (1 lb) ripe tomatoes

2 tablespoons olive oil

2 onions, chopped

2 garlic cloves, crushed

3 tablespoons tomato passata (puréed tomatoes)

2 large carrots, diced

2 celery stalks, trimmed and diced

1.7 litres (59 fl oz) vegetable or chicken stock

2 bay leaves

2 tablespoons lemon juice

30 g (1 oz) chopped flat leaf (Italian) parsley

SERVES 8

Put the beans in a bowl, cover with cold water and leave the beans to soak overnight.

Score a cross in the base of each tomato. Put in a heatproof bowl and cover with boiling water. Leave for 30 seconds then transfer to cold water and peel the skin away from the cross and roughly chop the flesh.

Drain the beans and rinse under cold water. Heat the oil in a 5 litre (175 fl oz/20 cup) saucepan. Add the onion, reduce the heat and cook gently for 10 minutes, stirring occasionally. Stir in the garlic and cook for 1 minute. Add the cannellini beans, chopped tomato, passata, carrot, celery and stock. Add the bay leaves and stir. Bring to the boil, then reduce the heat to medium-low and simmer, covered, for 45-60 minutes, or until the beans are tender.

Just before serving, stir in the lemon juice and season to taste. Stir in some of the parsley and use the rest as a garnish.

PREPARATION TIME: 20 MINUTES +   COOKING TIME: 1 HOUR 15 MINUTES

BREADS

SOURDOUGH RYE BREAD

SOURDOUGH STARTER
2 teaspoons dried yeast
1 teaspoon caster (superfine) sugar
200 g (7 oz/2 cups) rye flour

BREAD DOUGH
100 g (3½ oz/1 cup) rye flour
550 g (1 lb 4 oz/4½ cups) unbleached
plain (all-purpose) flour
45 g (1¾ oz/¼ cup) soft brown sugar
3 teaspoons caraway seeds
2 teaspoons dried yeast, extra
60 ml (2 fl oz/¼ cup) oil
rye flour, extra, to sprinkle

MAKES 2 LOAVES

To make the sourdough starter, combine the yeast, sugar, rye flour and 435 ml (15¼ fl oz/1¾ cups) warm water in a bowl. Cover with plastic wrap and set aside overnight at room temperature to sour. For a stronger flavour, leave for up to 3 days.

To make the bread dough, brush a large baking tray with oil or melted butter. In a large bowl, combine the rye flour, 440 g (15½ oz/3½ cups) of the plain flour, sugar, caraway seeds and 2 teaspoons salt. Dissolve the yeast in 250 ml (9 fl oz/1 cup) warm water. Make a well in the centre of the dry ingredients and add the sourdough starter, dissolved yeast and oil. Mix, using a wooden spoon then your hands, until the dough forms a rough, slightly sticky ball, which leaves the side of the bowl. Add some of the remaining flour, if necessary — you may not need to use it all.

Turn onto a lightly floured surface. Knead for 10 minutes, or until smooth and elastic. Incorporate the remaining flour, if needed. Place the dough in a large, lightly oiled bowl. Leave, covered with plastic wrap, in a warm place for 45 minutes, or until well risen. Punch down and knead for 1 minute. Divide into two even-sized portions. Shape into round or oblong loaves and place on the baking tray. Sprinkle with rye flour and use the end of a wooden spoon handle to press holes 2 cm (¾ inch) deep in the top, or make three slashes. Leave, covered with plastic wrap, in a warm place for 45 minutes, or until the dough is well risen.

Preheat the oven to 180°C (350°F/Gas 4). Sprinkle the loaves with flour. Bake for 40 minutes, or until a skewer inserted in the centre comes out clean. Cool on a wire rack.

PREPARATION TIME: 120 MINUTES +   COOKING TIME: 40 MINUTES

CHEESE AND CHIVE SCONES

250 g (9 oz/2 cups) self-raising flour
30 g (1 oz) butter, chopped
60 g (2¼ oz/½ cup) grated cheddar cheese
3 tablespoons shredded parmesan cheese
2 tablespoons snipped chives
125 ml (4 fl oz/½ cup) milk
3 tablespoons grated cheddar cheese, extra

MAKES 9

Preheat the oven to 210°C (415°F/Gas 6-7). Brush a baking tray with melted butter or oil. Sift the flour and a pinch of salt into a bowl. Rub in the butter using your fingertips. Stir in the cheeses and the chives. Make a well in the centre, add the milk and almost all of 125 ml (4 fl oz/½ cup) water. Mix lightly with a flat-bladed knife to form a soft dough, adding more water if the dough is too dry.

Knead the dough briefly on a lightly floured surface until smooth. Press out the dough to 2 cm (¾ inch) thick. Using a floured 5 cm (2 inch) plain round cutter, cut nine rounds from the dough. Place the rounds on the prepared tray and sprinkle with extra cheese. Bake for 12 minutes, or until the cheese is golden.

PREPARATION TIME: 20 MINUTES   COOKING TIME: 12 MINUTES

CLOVER LEAF ROLLS

2 teaspoons dried yeast
1 teaspoon caster (superfine) sugar
500 g (1 lb 2 oz) white strong flour
2 tablespoons dried whole milk powder
1 tablespoon caster (superfine) sugar, extra
60 ml (2 fl oz/¼ cup) vegetable oil

MAKES 16–24 ROLLS

Put the yeast, sugar and 125 ml (4 fl oz/½ cup) warm water in a small bowl and stir well to combine. Leave in a warm, draught-free place for 10 minutes, or until bubbles appear on the surface. The mixture should be frothy and slightly increased in volume.

Sift the flour, milk powder, extra sugar and 1 teaspoon salt into a large bowl. Make a well in the centre, add the yeast mixture, vegetable oil and 250 ml (9 fl oz/1 cup) warm water. Mix to a soft dough using a large metal spoon. The moisture content of flour can vary greatly between brands and even between batches so add extra water or flour, 1 tablespoon at a time, if the dough is too dry or too sticky. Do not add too much flour because the dough will absorb more flour during kneading.

Divide the dough into 16–24 even pieces. Divide each piece into three even-sized balls. Place the trio of balls from each piece close together on lightly oiled baking trays and 5 cm (2 inches) apart. Cover with plastic wrap and leave in a warm place for 20 minutes, or until well risen. Preheat the oven to 180°C (350°F/Gas 4). Brush the rolls with a glaze or topping. Bake for 15–20 minutes, or until risen and golden.

PREPARATION TIME: 40 MINUTES   COOKING TIME: 20 MINUTES

Cheese and chive scones

COTTAGE LOAF

2 teaspoons dried yeast
1 tablespoon soft brown sugar
250 g (9 oz/2 cups) white strong flour
300 g (10½ oz/2 cups) wholemeal
(wholewheat) strong flour
1 tablespoon vegetable oil

MAKES 1 LARGE LOAF

Put the yeast, 1 teaspoon of the sugar and 125 ml (4 fl oz/½ cup) warm water in a small bowl and mix well. Leave in a warm, draught-free place for 10 minutes, or until bubbles appear on the surface. The mixture should be frothy and slightly increased in volume.

Put the flours and 1 teaspoon salt in a large bowl. Make a well in the centre and add the yeast mixture, oil, the remaining sugar and 250 ml (9 fl oz/1 cup) warm water. Mix with a wooden spoon then turn out onto a lightly floured surface. Knead for 10 minutes, or until smooth and elastic. Incorporate a little extra flour into the dough as you knead, to stop the dough from sticking.

Place the dough in an oiled bowl and lightly brush oil over the dough. Cover with plastic wrap or a damp tea towel (dish towel) and leave in a warm place for 45 minutes, or until doubled in size.

Punch down the dough then turn out onto a lightly floured surface and knead the dough for 3-4 minutes. Pull away one-third of the dough and knead both portions into a smooth ball. Place the large ball on a large floured baking tray and brush the top with water. Sit the smaller ball on top and, using two fingers, press down into the centre of the dough to join the two balls together. Cover with plastic wrap or a damp tea towel and set aside in a warm place for 40 minutes, or until well risen.

Preheat the oven to 190°C (375°F/Gas 5). Sift some white flour over the top of the loaf and bake for 40 minutes, or until golden brown and cooked. Leave on the tray for 2-3 minutes to cool slightly, then turn out onto a wire rack to cool.

PREPARATION TIME: 30 MINUTES +   COOKING TIME: 40 MINUTES

BEER BREAD ROLLS

405 g (14¼ g/3¼ cups) plain (all-purpose) flour
3 teaspoons baking powder
1 tablespoon sugar
50 g (1¾ oz) butter, chopped
375 ml (13 fl oz/1½ cups) beer

MAKES 4

Process the flour, baking powder, sugar, butter and 1 teaspoon salt in a food processor until crumbly. Add the beer and process in bursts to form a soft dough.

Preheat the oven to 210°C (415°F/Gas 6-7). Turn the dough out onto a well-floured surface and knead until smooth, adding extra flour if needed. Divide the dough into four balls, place on greased oven trays and flatten slightly. Brush with a little water and slash the tops with a knife. Bake for 10 minutes. Reduce the oven to 180°C (350°F/Gas 4) and bake for about 10 minutes, or until cooked. Cool on a wire rack. Serve with butter.

PREPARATION TIME: 15 MINUTES   COOKING TIME: 20 MINUTES

PARATHAS

280 g (10 oz/2¼ cups) atta flour (see Note)
40 g (1½ oz) ghee
extra melted ghee or oil, to brush and for pan-frying

MAKES 10

Put the atta flour and a pinch of salt in a large bowl. Using your fingertips, rub in the ghee until fine and crumbly. Make a well in the centre and gradually add 185 ml (6 fl oz/¾ cup) cold water to form a firm dough.

Turn the dough out onto a well-floured surface and knead until smooth. Cover with plastic wrap and set aside for 40 minutes. Divide the dough into 10 equal portions. Roll each on a floured surface to form a 13 cm (5 inch) circle. Brush lightly with melted ghee. Cut from the centre of each round to the outer edge. Roll from one cut edge tightly to form a cone shape, then press down on the pointed top (doing this forms the traditional flaky layers of the bread). Re-roll into a 13 cm (5 inch) circle. Cook one at a time in hot ghee or oil in a frying pan for about 1 minute each side until puffed and lightly browned on both sides. Drain on paper towel.

PREPARATION TIME: 30 MINUTES   COOKING TIME: 20 MINUTES

NOTE: Paratha is a flaky, unleavened bread from India. Atta flour is a type of wholemeal flour traditionally used to make parathas.

Beer bread rolls

FOUGASSE

2 teaspoons dried yeast
1 teaspoon sugar
500 g (1 lb 2 oz/4 cups) white strong flour
60 ml (2 fl oz/¼ cup) olive oil
185 g (6½ oz/1 cup) black pitted olives, chopped (optional)
1 handful chopped mixed herbs, such as parsley, oregano and basil (optional)

MAKES 4 SMALL LOAVES

Put the yeast, sugar and 125 ml (4 fl oz/½ cup) warm water in a small bowl and stir until dissolved. Leave in a warm, draught-free place for 10 minutes, or until bubbles appear on the surface. The mixture should be frothy and slightly increased in volume.

Sift the flour and 2 teaspoons salt into a bowl and make a well in the centre. Add the yeast mixture, olive oil and 185 ml (6 fl oz/¾ cup) warm water. Mix to a soft dough and gather into a ball with floured hands. Turn out onto a floured surface and knead for 10 minutes, or until smooth. Place the dough in a large, lightly oiled bowl, cover loosely with plastic wrap or a damp tea towel (dish towel) and leave in a warm place for 1 hour, or until doubled in size.

Punch down the dough and add the olives and herbs, if desired. Knead for 1 minute. Divide the mixture into four equal portions. Press each portion into a large, oval shape about 1 cm (½ inch) thick and make several cuts on either side of each. Lay the dough on large, floured baking trays, cover with plastic wrap and leave to rise for 20 minutes.

Preheat the oven to 210°C (415°F/Gas 6-7). Bake the fougasse for 35 minutes, or until crisp. To make the crust crispy, spray the inside of the oven with water after 15 minutes cooking.

PREPARATION TIME: 30 MINUTES +   COOKING TIME: 35 MINUTES

NOTE: Although fougasse is traditionally made as a plain bread, these days bakeries often incorporate ingredients such as fresh herbs, olives, chopped ham and anchovies into the dough.

ONION AND BUTTERMILK BREAD

375 g (13 oz/3 cups) self-raising flour
35 g (1¼ oz) dried French onion soup
2 tablespoons snipped chives
435 ml (15¼ fl oz/1¾ cups) buttermilk, plus a little extra

MAKES 4 SMALL LOAVES

Preheat the oven to 180°C (350°F/Gas 4).

Sift the flour into a large bowl and stir in the dried soup and chives. Mix in the buttermilk with a flat-bladed knife, using a cutting action, until the mixture forms a soft dough. Add extra buttermilk if the mixture is too dry.

Turn the dough out onto a lightly floured surface and quickly knead into a smooth ball. Cut into four even-sized pieces and shape each into a ball. Place on a floured baking tray, allowing room for each to rise. Sift extra flour over the top and make a slash with a sharp knife across the top of each loaf. Bake the loaves for 25–30 minutes, or until cooked and golden.

PREPARATION TIME: 15 MINUTES   COOKING TIME: 30 MINUTES

HERB BREAD

125 g (4 oz) butter, softened
30 g (1 oz) chopped mixed herbs
1 garlic clove, finely chopped (optional)
1 baguette

SERVES 4

Preheat the oven to 180°C (350°F/Gas 4).

Combine the butter, mixed herbs and garlic, if using. Slice the baguette, diagonally, almost all the way through, and spread each piece with the herb butter. Reshape into a loaf, wrap in foil and bake for 20 minutes, or until the loaf is crisp and hot.

PREPARATION TIME: 10 MINUTES   COOKING TIME: 20 MINUTES

Onion and buttermilk bread

SCOTTISH BAPS

2 teaspoons dried yeast
1 teaspoon caster (superfine) sugar
440 g (15½ oz/3½ cups) white strong flour
250 ml (9 fl oz/1 cup) lukewarm milk
50 g (1¾ oz) butter, melted
1 tablespoon plain (all-purpose) flour

MAKES 12 BAPS

Lightly dust two baking trays with flour. Put the yeast, sugar and 2 tablespoons of the white strong flour in a small bowl. Gradually add the milk, blending until smooth and dissolved. Leave in a warm, draught-free place for 10 minutes, or until bubbles appear on the surface. The mixture should be frothy and slightly increased in volume.

Sift the remaining flour and 1½ teaspoons salt into a large bowl. Make a well in the centre and add the yeast mixture and butter. Using a flat-bladed knife, mix to form a soft dough. Turn the dough onto a lightly floured surface and knead for 3 minutes, or until smooth. Shape into a ball and place in a large oiled bowl. Cover with plastic wrap or a damp tea towel (dish towel) and leave in a warm place for 1 hour, or until well risen.

Preheat the oven to 210°C (415°F/Gas 6–7). Punch down the dough with your fist. Knead the dough again for 2 minutes, or until smooth. Divide into 12 pieces. Knead one portion at a time on a lightly floured surface for 1 minute, roll into a ball and shape into a flat oval. Repeat with the remaining dough.

Place the baps on the trays and dust with the plain flour. Cover with plastic wrap and leave in a warm place for 15 minutes, or until well risen. Make an indent in the centre of each bap with your finger. Bake for 30 minutes until browned and cooked through. Serve warm.

PREPARATION TIME: 40 MINUTES +   COOKING TIME: 30 MINUTES

LEMON PEPPER BREAD

250 g (9 oz/2 cups) self-raising flour
2 teaspoons lemon pepper, or 1 teaspoon grated lemon zest and 2 teaspoons black pepper
50 g (1³/₄ oz) butter, chopped
1 tablespoon snipped chives
90 g (3¹/₄ oz/³/₄ cup) grated cheddar cheese
2 teaspoons white vinegar
185 ml (6 fl oz/³/₄ cup) milk

MAKES 2 LOAVES

Preheat the oven to 210°C (415°F/Gas 6-7). Brush two baking trays with melted butter or oil. Sift the flour and 1 teaspoon salt into a large bowl and add the lemon pepper, or lemon zest and pepper. Using your fingertips, rub in the butter until the mixture resembles coarse breadcrumbs. Stir in the chives and cheese.

In a separate bowl, stir the vinegar into the milk (it should look slightly curdled). Add to the flour mixture and mix to a soft dough, adding more milk if dough is too stiff.

Turn the dough out onto a lightly floured surface and knead until smooth. Divide the dough into two portions. Place on the prepared trays and press each portion out into a circle approximately 2.5 cm (1 inch) thick. Score each with a knife into eight wedges, cutting lightly into the top of the bread. Dust lightly with flour. Bake for 20–25 minutes, or until the bread is a deep golden colour and sounds hollow when tapped on the base. Serve warm with butter.

PREPARATION TIME: 20 MINUTES   COOKING TIME: 25 MINUTES

CHEESY HERB ROLLS

125 g (4¹/₂ oz) butter, softened
1 tablespoon chopped basil
1 tablespoon chopped flat-leaf (Italian) parsley
1 tablespoon snipped chives
30 g (1 oz/1¹/₄ cups) grated cheddar cheese
4 crusty rosetta rolls

SERVES 4

Preheat the oven to 160°C (315°F/Gas 2-3). Combine the butter with the herbs and cheese and season. Cut the rolls into thin slices, but don't cut all the way through. Spread each side of each slice with the flavoured butter. Bake for 15 minutes, or until the rolls are crisp and golden.

PREPARATION TIME: 10 MINUTES   COOKING TIME: 15 MINUTES

Lemon pepper bread

MINI BAGUETTES

2 teaspoons dried yeast
1 teaspoon sugar
90 g (3¼ oz/¾ cup) plain (all-purpose) flour
375 g (13 oz/3 cups) white strong flour
2 tablespoons polenta, to sprinkle

MAKES 3 LOAVES

Put the yeast, sugar and 310 ml (10¾ fl oz/1¼ cups) warm water in a small bowl and mix well. Leave in a warm, draught-free place for 10 minutes, or until bubbles appear on the surface. The mixture should be frothy and slightly increased in volume.

Mix together the flours and ½ teaspoon salt and transfer half the dry ingredients to a large bowl. Make a well in the centre and add the yeast mixture. Using a large metal spoon fold the flour into the yeast mixture. This should form a soft dough. Cover the bowl with a damp tea towel (dish towel) or plastic wrap and set aside for 30–35 minutes, or until frothy and risen by about one third of its original size.

Mix in the remaining dry ingredients and add up to 60 ml (2 fl oz/¼ cup) warm water, enough to form a soft, but slightly sticky dough. Knead the dough on a lightly floured surface for about 10 minutes, or until smooth and elastic. If the dough sticks to the work surface while kneading, flour the surface sparingly, but try to avoid adding too much flour. Shape the dough into a ball and place in a large lightly greased bowl. Cover with a damp tea towel or plastic wrap and leave in a warm place for about 1 hour, until the dough has doubled in size.

Lightly grease two large baking trays and sprinkle with polenta. Punch down the dough and knead for 2–3 minutes. Divide the dough into three portions and press or roll each into a rectangle about 20 x 40 cm (8 x 16 inches). Roll each up firmly into a long sausage shape and place, seam side down, well spaced on the prepared trays. Cover loosely with a damp tea towel or plastic wrap and set aside in a warm place for 40 minutes, or until doubled in size.

Preheat the oven to 220°C (425°F/Gas 7). Lightly brush the loaves with water and make diagonal slashes across the top at 6 cm (2½ inch) intervals. Place the trays in the oven and spray the oven with water. Bake the bread for 20 minutes, spraying inside the oven with water twice during this time. Lower the temperature to 180°C (350°F/Gas 4) and bake for another 5–10 minutes, or until the crust is golden and firm and the base sounds hollow when tapped underneath. Cool on a wire rack. Baguettes are best eaten within a few hours of baking.

PREPARATION TIME: 25 MINUTES +   COOKING TIME: 30 MINUTES

POTATO AND OLIVE SCONES

250 g (9 oz) potatoes, chopped
125 ml (4 fl oz/½ cup) milk
250 g (9 oz/2 cups) self-raising flour
30 g (1 oz) butter, chopped
3 tablespoons black olives, pitted
and chopped
3–4 teaspoons chopped rosemary
milk, extra, to glaze

MAKES 15

Preheat the oven to 210°C (415°F/Gas 6–7). Brush a baking tray with melted butter or oil. Boil or microwave the potatoes until tender. Mash the potatoes with the milk and season with freshly ground black pepper.

Sift the flour into a large bowl. Rub in the butter, using your fingertips. Add the olives and rosemary and stir until just combined. Make a well in the centre and add the mashed potato and almost all of 125 ml (4 fl oz/½ cup) water. Mix with a flat-bladed knife, using a cutting action, until the mixture forms a soft dough. Add more water if the dough is too dry.

Knead the dough briefly on a lightly floured surface until smooth. Press out to a thickness of 2 cm (¾ inch). Using a floured 5 cm (2 inch) plain round cutter, cut 15 rounds from the dough and place them on the prepared tray. Brush the tops with the extra milk and cook for about 10–15 minutes until the scones are golden brown.

PREPARATION TIME: 25 MINUTES   COOKING TIME: 15 MINUTES

TORTILLAS

185 g (6½ oz/1½ cups) plain (all-purpose)
flour
150 g (5½ oz/1 cup) cornmeal

MAKES 16

Sift the flour and cornmeal into a large bowl. Make a well in the centre and then gradually add 250 ml (9 fl oz/1 cup) warm water. Mix to a firm dough with a flat-bladed knife. Turn out onto a lightly floured surface. Knead the dough for 5 minutes or until smooth.

Divide the dough into 16 portions. Roll out one portion on a lightly floured surface to a 20 cm (8 inch) round. Set aside, cover with plastic wrap and repeat with remaining portions.

Heat a heavy-based frying pan or hot plate. Place tortillas one at a time in the pan. When the edges begin to curl slightly, turn and cook the other side. A few seconds each side is ample cooking time. If residual flour begins to burn in the pan, wipe it out with paper towel.

PREPARATION TIME: 30 MINUTES   COOKING TIME: 20 MINUTES

Potato and olive scones

CHEESE AND HERB PULL-APART

2 teaspoons dried yeast
1 teaspoon sugar
500 g (1 lb 2 oz/4 cups) plain (all-purpose) flour
2 tablespoons chopped flat-leaf (Italian) parsley
2 tablespoons snipped chives
1 tablespoon chopped thyme
60 g (2¼ oz) cheddar cheese, grated
milk, to glaze

MAKES 1 LOAF

Put the yeast, sugar and 125 ml (4 fl oz/½ cup) warm water in a small bowl and stir well. Leave in a warm place for 10 minutes, or until bubbles appear on the surface. The mixture should be frothy and slightly increased in volume.

Sift the flour and 1½ teaspoons salt in a large bowl. Make a well in the centre and add the yeast mixture and 250 ml (9 fl oz/1 cup) warm water. Mix to a soft dough. Turn onto a lightly floured surface and knead for 10 minutes, or until smooth. Place the dough in an oiled bowl, cover with plastic wrap or a damp tea towel (dish towel) and leave for 1 hour, or until doubled in size.

Punch down the dough and knead for 1 minute. Divide the dough in half and shape each half into 10 flat discs, 6 cm (2½ inches) in diameter. Mix the herbs with the cheddar and put 2 teaspoons of the mixture on one of the discs. Press another disc on top, then repeat with the remaining discs and herb mixture.

Grease a 6 x 10.5 x 21 cm (2½ x 4¼ x 8¼ inch) loaf (bar) tin. Stand the filled discs upright in the prepared tin, squashing them together. Cover the tin with plastic wrap or a damp tea towel and leave in a warm place for 30 minutes, or until the dough is well risen.

Preheat the oven to 210°C (415°F/Gas 6-7). Lightly brush the loaf with a little milk and bake for 30 minutes, or until the bread is brown and crusty and sounds hollow when tapped on the base.

PREPARATION TIME: 30 MINUTES +   COOKING TIME: 30 MINUTES

MINI ONION AND PARMESAN SCONES

30 g (1 oz) butter
1 small onion, finely chopped
250 g (9 oz/2 cups) self-raising flour, sifted
50 g (1³/₄ oz/½ cup) finely shredded fresh parmesan cheese
125 ml (4 oz/½ cup) milk
cayenne pepper, to sprinkle

MAKES 24

Preheat the oven to 210°C (415°F/Gas 6–7). Brush a baking tray with a little melted butter or oil.

Melt the butter in a small frying pan, add the onion and cook, over low heat, for 2–3 minutes or until soft. Cool slightly.

Combine the sifted flour, parmesan and a pinch salt in a bowl. Make a well in the centre and add the onion. Combine the milk with 125 ml (4 oz/½ cup) water and add almost all to the bowl. Mix lightly, with a flat-bladed knife, using a cutting action, until the mixture forms a soft dough. Add more liquid if the dough is too dry. Knead dough briefly on a lightly floured surface until smooth and press out to 2 cm (³/₄ inch) thick. Cut the dough into 24 rounds with a 3 cm (1¹/₄ inch) plain round cutter. Place the rounds on the prepared tray and sprinkle each lightly with cayenne pepper. Cook for 10–12 minutes until golden brown.

PREPARATION TIME: 25 MINUTES   COOKING TIME: 12 MINUTES

NOTE: Handle scone dough with a light touch. Cut the liquid in with a knife and then take care not to over-knead or you'll have tough scones.

POPOVERS

250 g (9 oz/2 cups) plain (all-purpose) flour
4 eggs, lightly beaten
125 ml (4 oz/½ cup) pouring (whipping) cream
250 ml (9 oz/1 cup) milk
45 g (³/₄ oz) butter, melted

MAKES 12

Preheat the oven to 200°C (400°F/Gas 6). Put the flour in a food processor. With the machine running, add the eggs, cream, milk and butter and process until smooth. Pour into a jug.

Butter a 12-hole 125 ml (4 fl oz/1/2 cup) muffin tin and divide the mixture evenly among the holes. Place in the oven and bake for 35 minutes, or until the popovers are golden and puffy.

PREPARATION TIME: 5 MINUTES   COOKING TIME: 35 MINUTES

CIABATTA

2 teaspoons dried yeast
1 teaspoon sugar
375 g (13 oz/3 cups) white strong flour
50 ml (1³/4 fl oz) olive oil
extra flour, to sprinkle

MAKES 1 LOAF

Put the yeast, sugar and 80 ml (2½ oz/⅓ cup) warm water in a small bowl and stir well. Leave in a warm, draught-free place for 10 minutes, or until bubbles appear on the surface. The mixture should be frothy and slightly increased in volume.

Put 250 g (9 oz/2 cups) of the flour in a large bowl with 2 teaspoons salt and make a well in the centre. Add the yeast mixture, oil and 230 ml (7³/4 fl oz) water to the bowl and stir to combine. Use a cupped hand to knead the wet dough, lifting and stirring for 5 minutes. The dough will be quite wet at this stage. Shape the dough into a ball and put in a clean bowl. Cover with plastic wrap or a damp tea towel (dish towel) and leave in a warm place for 4 hours, or until doubled in size.

Stir in the remaining flour, using a cupped hand, and mix until the flour has been incorporated. Scrape down the side of the bowl. Cover with plastic wrap or a clean tea towel and leave in a warm place for 1–1¼ hours.

Liberally sprinkle a large baking tray with flour. Do not punch down the dough but carefully tip it out onto the tray. Use floured hands to spread the dough into an oval about 12 x 30 cm (4½ x 12 inches). Use heavily floured hands to spread evenly and tuck under the dough edges to plump up the dough. Sprinkle liberally with flour. Cover with plastic wrap and leave for 30 minutes.

Preheat the oven to 210°C (415°F/Gas 6–7). Place a heatproof container of ice on the base of the oven. Bake the ciabatta for 30 minutes, or until puffed and golden. Remove the melted ice after about 20 minutes. The loaf is cooked when it sounds hollow when tapped.

PREPARATION TIME: 30 MINUTES +   COOKING TIME: 30 MINUTES

CAPSICUM AND CORN MUFFINS

125 g (4½ oz/1 cup) plain (all-purpose) flour
1 tablespoon baking powder
150 g (5½ oz/1 cup) fine polenta
1 tablespoon caster (superfine) sugar
1 egg
170 ml (5½ fl oz/⅔ cup) milk
¼ teaspoon Tabasco sauce (optional)
60 ml (2 fl oz/¼ cup) oil
½ red capsicum (pepper), seeded, membrane removed and finely chopped
440 g (15½ oz) tinned corn kernels, drained
3 tablespoons finely chopped flat-leaf (Italian) parsley

MAKES 12

Preheat the oven to 210°C (415°F/Gas 6–7). Brush a 12-hole muffin tin with oil or melted butter. Sift the flour, baking powder and ¼ teaspoon salt into a large bowl. Add the polenta and sugar. Stir thoroughly until all the ingredients are well mixed. Make a well in the centre.

Combine the egg, milk, Tabasco and oil in a separate bowl. Add the egg mixture, capsicum, corn and parsley all at once to the dry ingredients. Stir quickly with a wooden spoon or rubber spatula until all the ingredients are just moistened. (Do not over-mix — the batter should be quite lumpy.)

Spoon the mixture into the tin. Bake for 20 minutes, or until golden. Loosen with a knife but leave in the tin for 2 minutes. Cool on a wire rack.

PREPARATION TIME: 15 MINUTES   COOKING TIME: 20 MINUTES

LAYERED COB

2 red capsicums (peppers), seeded, membrane removed and cut into large pieces
500 g (1 lb 2 oz) eggplant (aubergine)
400 g (14 oz) baby English spinach, trimmed
22 cm (8½ inch) cob (round) loaf
2 tablespoons oil
2 garlic cloves, crushed
500 g (1 lb 2 oz/2 cups) ricotta cheese
2 tablespoons chopped flat-leaf (Italian) parsley
25 g (1 oz/¼ cup) freshly grated parmesan cheese
150 g (5½ oz) sliced ham

SERVES 6–8

Cook the capsicum, skin side up, under a hot grill (broiler) until the skins blacken and blister. Cool in a plastic bag, then peel and slice the flesh. Cut the eggplant into 1 cm (½ inch) slices and grill until golden on both sides. Steam the spinach briefly until wilted, then cool and squeeze out any excess liquid.

Cut a large round from the top of the cob loaf and reserve. Scoop out the white bread, leaving a 1 cm (½ inch) border. Combine the oil and garlic and brush the insides of the loaf and lid.

Combine the ricotta, parsley and parmesan in a bowl. Place half the eggplant slices in the loaf, layer the capsicum on top, then the ham. Top with the ricotta mixture and season. Spread the spinach leaves over the top, then add the remaining eggplant. Put the 'lid' on and wrap tightly with plastic wrap. Place a plate on top, weigh down with tins and chill overnight. Serve hot or cold in wedges. To heat, wrap in foil and bake in a 200°C (400°F/Gas 6) oven for 15–20 minutes.

PREPARATION TIME: 45 MINUTES +   COOKING TIME: 10 MINUTES

Capsicum and corn muffins

BAGELS

2 teaspoons dried yeast
1 teaspoon sugar
1 tablespoon barley malt syrup or honey
500 g (1 lb 2 oz/4 cups) white strong flour
2 teaspoons salt
coarse polenta, to dust

MAKES 8

Put the yeast, sugar and 375 ml (13 fl oz/1½ cups) warm water in a small bowl and stir until dissolved. Leave in a warm place for 10 minutes, or until bubbles appear on the surface. The mixture should be frothy and slightly increased in volume.

Put 250 g (9 oz/2 cups) of the flour in a large bowl, make a well in the centre and add the yeast mixture and salt. Stir with a wooden spoon, adding flour as necessary to make a firm dough. Turn out onto a floured work surface and knead for 10–12 minutes, or until smooth and stiff. Add more flour if necessary, to make the dough quite stiff, then divide into eight portions and roll them into smooth balls. Cover with plastic wrap or a clean tea towel (dish towel) and leave for 5 minutes.

Roll each ball under your palms to form a rope 28 cm (11¼ inches) long. Do not taper the ends of the rope. Dampen the ends slightly, overlap by 4 cm (1½ inches) and pinch firmly together. Place one at a time around the base of your fingers and, with the overlap under your palm, roll the rope several times. Apply firm pressure to seal the seam. It should be the same thickness all the way around. Place all the balls on polenta-dusted baking trays, cover with plastic wrap and refrigerate for 12 hours.

Preheat the oven to 240°C (475°F/Gas 8). Line two baking trays with baking paper. Remove the bagels from the fridge 20 minutes before baking. Bring a large saucepan of water to the boil and drop the bagels, in batches of three or four, into the water for 30 seconds. Remove and drain, base-down, on a wire rack.

Place the bagels on the baking trays and bake for 15 minutes, or until deep golden brown and crisp. Cool on a wire rack.

PREPARATION TIME: 35 MINUTES +   COOKING TIME: 16 MINUTES

TRADITIONAL CORN BREAD

150 g (5½ oz/1 cup) polenta
2 tablespoons caster (superfine) sugar
125 g (4½ oz/1 cup) plain (all-purpose) flour
2 teaspoons baking powder
½ teaspoon bicarbonate of soda (baking soda)
1 egg, lightly beaten
250 ml (9 fl oz/1 cup) buttermilk
60 g (2¼ oz) butter, melted

MAKES 1 LOAF

Preheat the oven to 210°C (415°F/Gas 6–7). Brush a 20 cm (8 inch) square cake tin with oil or melted butter and line the base with baking paper.

Put the polenta and sugar in a large bowl. Add the sifted flour, baking powder, bicarbonate of soda and ½ teaspoon salt and mix thoroughly.

In a separate bowl, combine the beaten egg, buttermilk and melted butter. Stir the mixture quickly into the dry ingredients. Stir only until the ingredients are moistened. Pour the mixture into the prepared tin and smooth the surface. Bake for 20–25 minutes, or until a skewer inserted in the centre of the bread comes out clean.

Place on a wire rack and leave to cool for 10 minutes before turning out. Cut into squares and serve warm.

PREPARATION TIME: 15 MINUTES   COOKING TIME: 25 MINUTES

CHAPATTIS

310 g (11 oz/2½ cups) fine wholemeal (whole-wheat) flour
1 tablespoon oil
60 g (2¼ oz/½ cup) fine wholemeal (whole-wheat) flour, extra

MAKES 20

Place the flour and 1 teaspoon salt in a large mixing bowl. Make a well in the centre. Add the oil and 250 ml (9 fl oz/1 cup) warm water all at once and use a wooden spoon, then your hands, to mix to a firm dough. Turn onto a lightly floured surface and knead for 15 minutes. Do not add the extra flour at this stage. Form dough into a smooth ball and place in a bowl. Cover with plastic wrap and set aside for at least 2 hours or overnight.

Divide the dough into 20 even-sized pieces. Form each piece into a smooth ball. With the aid of the extra flour, roll each ball into a thin, pancake-sized circle. Cover each chapatti with floured plastic wrap and leave to rest while rolling the remaining dough.

Heat a heavy-based frying pan until hot. Cook each chapatti for 1 minute, then turn and cook the other side for another minute. Adjust the heat so that the dough browns but does not burn. While the chapatti is cooking, press the edges with a folded tea towel (dish towel). This will help bubbles to form and make the chapatti lighter. Stack and wrap the cooked chapattis in a clean tea towel to keep them warm and soft. Serve immediately.

PREPARATION TIME: 40 MINUTES +   COOKING TIME: 40 MINUTES

Traditional corn bread

WALNUT BREAD

2½ teaspoons dried yeast

90 g (3¼ oz/¼ cup) liquid malt

2 tablespoons olive oil

300 g (10½ oz/3 cups) walnut halves, lightly toasted

540 g (1 lb 3 oz/4⅓ cups) white strong flour

1 egg, lightly beaten

MAKES 1 LOAF

Grease a baking tray. Put the yeast, liquid malt and 330 ml (11¼ fl oz/1⅓ cups) warm water in a small bowl and stir well. Leave in a warm, draught-free place for 10 minutes, or until bubbles appear on the surface. The mixture should be frothy and slightly increased in volume. Stir in the oil.

Process 200 g (7 oz/2 cups) of the walnuts in a food processor until they resemble coarse meal. Combine 500 g (1 lb 2 oz/4 cups) of the flour with 1½ teaspoons salt in a large bowl and stir in the walnut meal. Make a well and add the yeast mixture. Mix with a large metal spoon until just combined. Turn out onto a lightly floured surface and knead for 10 minutes, or until smooth, incorporating enough of the remaining flour to keep the dough from sticking — it should be soft and moist, but it won't become very springy. Shape the dough into a ball. Place in a lightly oiled bowl, cover with plastic wrap or a damp tea towel (dish towel) and leave in a warm place for up to 1½ hours, or until doubled in size.

Punch down the dough and turn out onto a lightly floured surface. With very little kneading, shape the dough into a flattened 20 x 25 cm (8 x 10 inch) rectangle. Spread with the remaining walnuts and roll up firmly from the short end. Place the loaf on the baking tray, cover with plastic wrap or a damp tea towel and leave to rise for 1 hour, or until doubled in size.

Preheat the oven to 190°C (375°F /Gas 5). Glaze the loaf with the egg and bake for 45-50 minutes, or until golden and hollow sounding when tapped. Transfer to a wire rack to cool.

PREPARATION TIME: 45 MINUTES +   COOKING TIME: 50 MINUTES

NOTE: Use good-quality pale and plump walnuts as cheaper varieties can be bitter.

ZUCCHINI AND CARROT MUFFINS

2 zucchinis (courgettes)
2 carrots
250 g (9 oz/2 cups) self-raising flour
1 teaspoon ground cinnamon
1/2 teaspoon freshly grated nutmeg
60 g (2 1/4 oz/1/2 cup) chopped pecans
4 eggs
250 ml (9 fl oz/1 cup) milk
90 g (3 1/4 oz) butter, melted

MAKES 12

Preheat the oven to 210°C (415°F/Gas 6–7). Brush a 12-hole muffin tin with melted butter or oil. Grate the zucchinis and carrots. Sift the flour, cinnamon, nutmeg and a pinch of salt into a large bowl. Add the carrot, zucchini and chopped pecans. Stir thoroughly until all the ingredients are well combined.

Combine the eggs, milk and melted butter in a separate bowl and whisk well until combined.

Make a well in the centre of the flour mixture and add the egg mixture all at once. Mix quickly with a fork or rubber spatula until all the ingredients are just moistened. (Do not over-mix — the batter should be quite lumpy.)

Spoon the batter evenly into the prepared tin. Bake for 15–20 minutes, or until golden. Loosen the muffins with a flat-bladed knife or spatula and leave in the tin for 2 minutes, before turning out onto a wire rack to cool.

PREPARATION TIME: 20 MINUTES   COOKING TIME: 20 MINUTES

PURIS

375 g (13 oz/2 1/2 cups) wholemeal (whole-wheat) flour
1 tablespoon ghee or oil
oil, for frying

MAKES 18

Sift the wholemeal flour with a pinch of salt. Using your fingertips, rub in the ghee. Gradually add 250 ml (9 oz/1 cup) water to form a firm dough. Knead on a lightly floured surface until smooth. Cover with plastic wrap and set aside for 50 minutes.

Divide the dough into 18 portions and roll each into a 14 cm (5 1/2 inch) circle. Heat 3 cm (1 1/4 inches) oil in a deep frying pan until moderately hot. Fry one puri at a time, spooning oil over until they puff up and swell. Cook on each side until golden brown. Drain on paper towel. Serve immediately.

PREPARATION TIME: 15 MINUTES   COOKING TIME: 25 MINUTES

NOTE: A puri is a traditional Indian bread, much like a deep-fried chapati, which puffs and swells as it cooks.

Zucchini and carrot muffins

POTATO BREAD

2 teaspoons dried yeast
500 g (1 lb 2 oz/4 cups) unbleached plain
(all-purpose) flour
2 tablespoons full-cream milk powder
235 g (8½ oz/1 cup) warm cooked mashed
potato
25 g (1 oz) snipped chives
1 egg white, to glaze
2 teaspoons cold water
sunflower seeds and pepitas (pumpkin
seeds), to sprinkle

MAKES 1 LOAF

Lightly grease a 25 cm (10 inch) round cake tin and line the base with baking paper. Put the yeast and 60 ml (2 fl oz/¼ cup) warm water in a small bowl and stir well. Leave in a warm, draught-free place for 10 minutes, or until bubbles appear on the surface. The mixture should be frothy and slightly increased in volume.

Sift 440 g (15½ oz/3½ cups) of the flour, the milk powder and 1 teaspoon salt into a large bowl. Using a fork, mix the potato and chives through the dry ingredients. Add the yeast mixture and 250 ml (9 fl oz/1 cup) warm water and mix until combined. Add enough of the remaining flour to make a soft dough.

Turn the dough onto a lightly floured surface. Knead for 10 minutes, or until the dough is smooth and elastic. Place in an oiled bowl, then brush the surface with oil. Cover with plastic wrap and leave in a warm place for 1 hour, or until well risen.

Punch down the dough, then knead for 1 minute. Divide into 12 equal pieces and form each piece into a smooth ball. Place evenly spaced balls in a daisy pattern in the tin, piling two balls in the centre. Cover with plastic wrap and leave to rise for 45 minutes, or until the dough has risen to the top of the tin. Preheat the oven to 210°C (415°F/Gas 6-7).

Brush the top with the combined egg white and water and sprinkle the sunflower seeds and pepitas over the top. Bake for 15 minutes. Reduce the oven to 180°C (350°F/Gas 4) and bake for another 20 minutes, or until a skewer inserted into the centre of the loaf comes out clean. Leave for 10 minutes, then turn out onto a wire rack.

PREPARATION TIME: 45 MINUTES +   COOKING TIME: 35 MINUTES

NOTE: Depending on the moisture content of the potato, extra flour may have to be added to make a soft, slightly sticky dough. The bread will keep for 3 days in an airtight container.

MOROCCAN FLATBREAD

375 g (13 oz/2½ cups) wholemeal
(whole-wheat) flour
1 teaspoon caster (superfine) sugar
2 teaspoons dried yeast
½ teaspoon sweet paprika
50 g (1¾ oz/⅓ cup) cornmeal
1 tablespoon oil
1 egg, lightly beaten
2 tablespoons sesame seeds

MAKES 16

Preheat the oven to 180°C (350°F/Gas 4). Lightly grease a baking tray. Put 75 g (2¾ oz/½ cup) of the flour, the sugar, yeast, 1 teaspoon salt and 310 ml (10¾ fl oz/1¼ cups) lukewarm water in a bowl and stir until dissolved. Cover and leave in a warm, draught-free place for 10 minutes, or until bubbles appear on the surface. The mixture should be frothy and slightly increased in volume.

Sift the paprika, cornmeal and remaining flour into a bowl. Add the oil then stir in the yeast mixture. Mix to a firm dough and knead until smooth. Cover and leave in a warm, draught-free place for 20 minutes.

Divide the dough into 16 portions, roll each into a ball then flatten into 8 cm (3¼ inch) rounds. Place on the baking tray, brush with egg and sprinkle with sesame seeds. Cover and set aside for 10 minutes, or until puffed up. Bake for 12 minutes, or until golden.

PREPARATION TIME: 1 HOUR +   COOKING TIME: 12 MINUTES

CORN BREAD

125 g (4½ oz/1 cup) self-raising flour
150 g (5½ oz/1 cup) fine cornmeal
1 egg
250 ml (9 fl oz/1 cup) buttermilk
60 ml (2 fl oz/¼ cup) oil

MAKES 1 LOAF

Preheat the oven to 220°C (425°F/Gas 7). Generously grease a 20 cm (8 inch) cast-iron frying pan with an ovenproof or removable handle, or round cake tin, with oil. Place in the oven to heat while making the batter.

Sift the flour into a bowl, add the cornmeal and 1 teaspoon salt and make a well in the centre. Whisk together the egg, buttermilk and oil, add to the dry ingredients and stir until just combined. Do not overbeat.

Pour into the hot cast-iron pan or cake tin and bake for 25 minutes, or until firm to the touch and golden brown. Serve, cut into wedges, warm or at room temperature.

PREPARATION TIME: 20 MINUTES   COOKING TIME: 25 MINUTES

Moroccan flatbread

PUMPERNICKEL

1 tablespoon dried yeast
1 teaspoon caster (superfine) sugar
90 g (3¼ oz/¼ cup) molasses
60 ml (2 fl oz/¼ cup) cider vinegar
90 g (3¼ oz) butter
30 g (1 oz) dark chocolate, chopped
1 tablespoon instant coffee powder
560 g (1 lb 4 oz/4½ cups) unbleached
plain (all-purpose) flour
300 g (10½ oz/3 cups) rye flour
75 g (2¾ oz/1 cup) bran
1 tablespoon caraway seeds
2 teaspoons fennel seeds
1 egg white
caraway seeds, extra, to sprinkle

MAKES 2 LOAVES

Grease a 20 cm (8 inch) round cake tin and a 12 x 28 cm (4½ x 11¼ inch) loaf (bar) or bread tin, or use any baking tin that has a 1.75 litre capacity. Line the base of each tin with baking paper. Put 125 ml (4 fl oz/½ cup) warm water, the yeast and sugar in a small bowl and stir well. Leave in a warm, draught-free place for 10 minutes, or until bubbles appear on the surface. The mixture should be frothy and slightly increased in volume.

Put the molasses, vinegar, butter, chocolate, coffee powder and 500 ml (17 fl oz/2 cups) cold water into a saucepan and stir over low heat until the butter and chocolate have melted and the mixture is just warmed.

Put the rye flour, bran, caraway and fennel seeds, 440 g (15½ oz/3½ cups) of the plain flour and 1 teaspoon salt in a large bowl. Make a well in the centre and add the yeast and chocolate mixtures. Using a wooden spoon, and then your hands, combine the dough until it leaves the side of the bowl and forms a firm, sticky ball.

Turn out onto a heavily floured surface and knead for 10 minutes. Incorporate enough of the remaining plain flour to make a dense but smooth and elastic dough. Divide in half and place in separate lightly oiled bowls. Brush the surface of the dough with melted butter or oil. Cover with plastic wrap or a damp tea towel (dish towel) and leave in a warm, draught-free place for 1¼ hours, or until well risen. Punch down the dough and knead each portion for 1 minute. Shape each portion to fit a tin and place one in each tin. Cover with lightly oiled plastic wrap or a damp tea towel and leave in a warm place for 1 hour, or until well risen.

Preheat the oven to 180°C (350°F/Gas 4). Glaze the dough with combined egg white and 1 tablespoon water and sprinkle with caraway seeds. Bake for 50 minutes, or until well browned. During the last 15 minutes, cover with foil to prevent excess browning. Leave in the tins for 15 minutes before turning out onto a wire rack to cool.

PREPARATION TIME: 1 HOUR +   COOKING TIME: 50 MINUTES

NOTE: Pumpernickel is a dense rye bread that originated in Germany.

MINI WHOLEMEAL LOAVES

2 teaspoons dried yeast
1 tablespoon caster (superfine) sugar
125 ml (4 fl oz/½ cup) warm milk
600 g (1 lb 5 oz/4 cups) wholemeal
(whole-wheat) strong flour
60 ml (2 fl oz/¼ cup) oil
1 egg, lightly beaten

MAKES 4 SMALL LOAVES

Grease four 13 x 6½ x 5 cm (5 x 2¾ x 2 inch) baking tins. Put the yeast, sugar and milk in a small bowl and mix well. Leave in a warm, draught-free place for 10 minutes, or until bubbles appear on the surface. The mixture should be frothy and slightly increased in volume.

Put the flour and 1 teaspoon salt in a large bowl, make a well in the centre and add the yeast mixture, oil and 250 ml (9 fl oz/1 cup) warm water. Mix to a soft dough and gather into a ball. Turn out onto a floured surface and knead for 10 minutes. Add a little extra flour if the dough is too sticky.

Place the dough in a large oiled bowl, cover loosely with plastic wrap or a damp tea towel (dish towel) and leave in a warm place for 1 hour, or until well risen. Punch down the dough, turn out onto a floured surface and knead for 1 minute, or until smooth. Divide into four portions, knead into shape and put in the tins. Cover loosely with plastic wrap or a damp tea towel and leave in a warm place for 45 minutes, or until risen.

Preheat the oven to 210°C (415°F/Gas 6–7). Brush the loaf tops with the beaten egg. Bake for 10 minutes, then reduce the oven temperature to 180°C (350°F/Gas 4) and bake for a further 30–35 minutes, or until the base sounds hollow when tapped. Cover with foil if the tops become too brown.

PREPARATION TIME: 40 MINUTES +   COOKING TIME: 45 MINUTES

PRETZELS

1 teaspoon dried yeast
¼ teaspoon sugar
150 ml (5 fl oz) warm milk
185 g (6½ oz/1½ cups) white strong flour
30 g (1 oz) butter, melted
1 egg yolk, lightly beaten
coarse sea salt, to sprinkle

MAKES 12

Put the yeast, sugar and warm milk in a small bowl and stir well. Leave in a warm, draught-free place for 10 minutes, or until bubbles appear on the surface. The mixture should be frothy and slightly increased in volume.

Put the flour and ¼ teaspoon salt in a large bowl and make a well in the centre. Add the yeast mixture and butter and mix to a rough dough with a wooden spoon. Turn out onto a floured surface and knead for 10 minutes until smooth and elastic.

Place into an oiled bowl, oil the surface of the dough, cover with plastic wrap or a clean tea towel (dish towel) and set aside in a warm place for 1 hour until doubled in size.

Preheat the oven to 190°C (375°F/Gas 5). Line a large baking tray with baking paper. Punch down the dough and knead again for 2–3 minutes. Divide into 12 pieces. Cover the dough while working with each piece. Roll each piece into a long rope 40 cm (16 inches) long. Circle and knot into a pretzel shape. Place well spaced on the tray. Cover with a tea towel. Leave to rise in a warm, draught-free place for 20–30 minutes.

Lightly brush the pretzels with the beaten egg yolk and sprinkle with sea salt. Place the pretzels in the oven and spray them twice with water before baking for 12–15 minutes, or until crisp and golden brown. Transfer to a wire rack to cool.

PREPARATION TIME: 50 MINUTES +   COOKING TIME: 15 MINUTES

MALT BREAD

2 teaspoons dried yeast
1 teaspoon sugar
300 g (10½ oz/2 cups) plain (all-purpose)
wholemeal (whole-wheat) flour
125 g (4½ oz/1 cup) plain (all-purpose)
flour
2 teaspoons ground cinnamon
55 g (2¼ oz/¼ cup) raisins
30 g (1 oz) butter, melted
1 tablespoon treacle
1 tablespoon liquid malt extract
1 tablespoon hot milk
½ teaspoon liquid malt extract, extra

MAKES 1 LOAF

Brush a 7 x 14 x 21 cm (2¾ x 5½ x 8¼ inch) loaf (bar) tin with oil and line the base with baking paper. Combine 250 ml (9 fl oz/1 cup) lukewarm water, the yeast and sugar in a small bowl. Cover with plastic wrap and set aside in a warm place for 10 minutes, or until bubbles appear on the surface. The mixture should be frothy and slightly increased in volume.

Sift the flours and cinnamon into a large bowl, then add the raisins and stir. Make a well in the centre. Add the melted butter, treacle, 1 tablespoon of malt extract and the yeast mixture. Mix to a soft dough using a flat-bladed knife. Turn onto a lightly floured surface and knead for 10 minutes, or until smooth. Shape the dough into a ball and place in a lightly oiled bowl. Set aside, covered with plastic wrap, in a warm place for 1 hour, or until well risen. Punch down the dough, then knead until smooth.

Roll into a 20 cm (8 inch) square and then roll up. Place the dough in the tin, with the seam underneath, and set aside, covered with plastic wrap, in a warm place for 40 minutes, or until well risen.

Preheat the oven to 180°C (350°F/Gas 4). Brush the dough with the combined milk and extra malt. Bake for 40 minutes or until a skewer inserted into the centre of the bread comes out clean. Set aside for 3 minutes in the tin before transferring to a wire rack to cool.

PREPARATION TIME: 45 MINUTES +   COOKING TIME: 40 MINUTES

INDEX

INDEX